The Great Physician:
The Healing Stories in Luke and Their Meaning for Today

by Lindsey P. Pherigo

And Jesus answered them, "Those who are well have no need of a physician, but those who are sick; I have not come to call the righteous, but sinners to repentance." (Luke 5:31-32)

HEALTH EXISTS WHEN BODY, MIND, AND SPIRIT WORK IN HARMONY

Published by
The Education and Cultivation Division
for
The Women's Division
General Board of Global Ministries
The United Methodist Church

Published in the United States of America

Library of Congress Catalog Card No: 82-084674

Please send any comments or critiques about the text and/or the teacher's guide to Literature Editor, Room 1356, General Board of Global Ministries, The United Methodist Church, 475 Riverside Drive, New York, N.Y. 10115.

Acknowledgements

My greatest debts are to my two editors: I gladly credit them for whatever readability this final product possesses. My official editor, Nancy A. Carter, has been patient beyond all expectations with the delays caused by my unexpected open-heart surgery just at the time the first draft was scheduled for completion. In addition to her patience, she has made several skillful arrangements of materials that greatly clarified what I wanted to say. My unofficial editor, Rebecca Hoge, has worked over the entire manuscript with me, in all of its drafts, exposing mannerisms I was unaware of, systematically changing passive verb forms to active, flagging unnecessary prejudices and personal opinions that violated my aim to be non-judgmental and helping me break the material into meaningful units.

I owe substantial debts to several others. Susan Halverstadt read the entire manuscript from the perspective of her expertise in health matters, helped with discussion options, and contributed many helpful suggestions. Two women were of special help from a religious and educational perspective. Frances Manson, associate pastor at Indian Heights United Methodist Church in Overland Park, Kansas, raised my consciousness level on several matters of common prejudice. Carole Mehl, Director of Christian Education at Central United Methodist Church in Kansas City, Missouri, brought some of the more abstract material down to earth, and at the same time raised some deeper questions than I could handle. Richard Athey, psychological counsellor at The Village Church in Prairie Village, Kansas, saved me some embarrassment by correcting several slips. Physician Max Miller, also of Village Church, provided me with valuable data about "spontaneous remissions" as understood in the medical world. Criticisms and suggestions from individual members of the Committees on Program and Spiritual and Theological Concerns of the Women's Division, which read each draft, have made the work stronger in every way.

Many others have given me the encouragement and support I needed to get myself deeply involved in an aspect of the Gospel of Luke that I had not previously explored in depth. Among these my colleague at Village Church, Rena Yocom, Minister of Adult Education, stands out clearly. More in the background are many adults in my classes at Village Church who were willing to hear and react to the ideas I had at the beginning of this research: their names are legion.

A special note of appreciation is due my long-suffering wife, Viola. This project has taken many, many hours out of the time we ordinarily spend together. Her complaints are justified, and yet she shares in my sense of accomplishment and has co-operated at every stage with generous understanding and full support.

December 29, 1982
Kansas City, Missouri

Contents

Acknowledgements...iii

Foreword... vii

1. Introduction to the Gospel According to Luke............1
   What Is the Gospel of Luke?......................................1
   Why Was It Written?... 2
   When Was It Written?..3
   Who Wrote It?.. 3
   How Was It Written?... 4
   What Is Its Viewpoint?..5
   What Is Its Structure?... 6
   What Are Its Additional Concerns?............................6
   The Focus of This Study...7

2. The Unity of Religion and Health...............................9
   Jesus' Holistic Ministry...9
   The Unity of Greek Medicine.................................. 11
   Early Christian Traditions..13
   The Loss of Holism in Protestantism....................... 14
   The Recovery of Unity... 16
   The Wholeness of Life... 17

3. The Role of Faith... 21
   The Healings of Jesus.. 21
   Whose Faith Is Needed?.. 23
   Different Concepts of Faith...................................... 25
   Is Faith Essential?... 27
   Faith Is a Gift.. 28

4. The Role of Touch... 29
   How Jesus Used Touch.. 29
   The Healer as Agent... 31
   A Modern Alternative..32
   Informal Touching...34
   Laying on of Hands.. 36

5. The Role of Prayer.. 37
   How Jesus Used Prayer... 37
   What Is Prayer?.. 38
   How We Pray..40
   Group Prayer..41
   Experimental Prayer..41
   Prayers for Healing... 43

6. The Role of the Word.. 45
   How Jesus Used the Word...................................... 45
   How the Disciples Used the Word........................... 47
   Presupposed World-Views......................................48
   Are Demons Real?... 49
   Another Kind of Healing Word...............................52

7. The Role of the Healer...54
   Jesus as Healer.. 54
   The Jewish Viewpoint..54
   The Greek Viewpoint.. 56
   The Power in a Healer...57
   Modern Research.. 59
   Becoming a Healer.. 63

8. The Role of Malady... 65
   The Universality of Malady.................................... 65
   The Old Hebrew View of Malady............................ 66
   Another Biblical View... 67
   Malady and Healing in Antiquity............................ 69
   Shamanism.. 70
   Modern Views of Malady..72
   The "New Age" Visions in Scripture........................ 74
   The Difficult Questions... 76

9. Technique or Grace?.. 77
   The Natural Laws of Health.................................... 77
   Healing As the Gift of God.................................... 79
   What We Can Do.. 82
   The Two Graces..82
   Other Explanations for Healing.............................. 84

10. Wholeness and Health... 86
   The Wholeness of Individuals................................. 86
   The Wholeness of Society...................................... 90
   What We Can Do.. 94

   Bibliography.. 95

   Teacher's Guide by Nancy A. Carter...................... 98

   Glossary..135

Foreword

All of the early Christian tradition about Jesus in his earthly life remember him as one vitally concerned about the total well-being of individuals. The Gospels stress his reputation as a healer. Luke's Gospel gives special attention to the concern of Jesus for total health. This book is a special study of the healing stories in that Gospel with a focus on the wholeness of life, the healing ministry of Jesus, and the interactions between spiritual, physical, and mental health.

At each point, this study reaches beyond the study of Luke's healing stories into the present world of spiritual healing. The dynamic behind first century healings and those of our time is probably identical in principle, even if first century explanations differ from ours. We will study several aspects of this dynamic.

It is characteristic of our time that "respectable" mainline churches—including most United Methodist churches—do not take the total healing ministry of the church seriously. We tend to separate spiritual matters from physical and to refer problems of physical health to the medical world. I intend in this study to give us a chance to reconsider this present practice and perhaps to revise it in the light of the ministry of Jesus as found in the Gospel of Luke.

In this book, the term "spiritual healing" stresses a healing dimension different from healing through medical and surgical procedures but one that is intimately related to it. I do not intend to set up tension between the two; both are needed.

I urge the reader to study carefully all the biblical passages on which the discussion is based. Different translations will shed new light on these key passages, but I have chosen to quote from the Revised Standard Version as the one most widely used today. Among other versions, I recommend the New English Bible, the Jerusalem Bible, Today's English Version, and Clarence Jordan's paraphrase, the Cotton Patch Version.

I have scattered discussion questions, or questions to think about, throughout the text. Rather than gathering them together at the end of each chapter, I have added them at the most relevant places in little boxes.

My mood is intended to be informational, not judgmental. Many "unusual" ideas characterize the literature on spiritual healing. These ideas are sometimes based on inaccurate information or fail to consider all the data available. I have found it difficult to weed these out. Some readers may feel I need to do more weeding. I have intentionally risked being too inclusive rather than too exclusive to leave the reader more broadly informed.

After the introductory chapters on the Gospel of Luke and on the unity of religion and health, I have treated the principal factors in spiritual healing in separate chapters on "The Role of..." These factors are Faith, Touch, Prayer, the Word, and the Healer. In each of these chapters, the beginning point is drawn from those healing stories in Luke that emphasize that particular factor. Then we will examine the modern understanding(s) of that particular factor. After considering these individual factors, we will recognize the positive role that illness sometimes plays in our lives (in "The Role of Malady"). Here also the relevant parts of Luke begin the discussion. The next chapter, "Technique or Grace?" raises significant theological concerns which bear directly on the whole focus of the study. A final chapter brings the previous material together under the theme of wholeness, both individual and societal, and applies it to our regular church life. This chapter takes its base from Luke's healing stories.

A wise word from Francis MacNutt is appropriate for this study book. "Those who want simple answers and absolute clarity are bound to be disappointed.... There will always be a mystery."[1]

---

[1]Francis MacNutt, *Healing* (1974; rpt. New York: Bantam Books, 1980), p. 119.

1

Introduction to the Gospel According to Luke

Readings from Luke and Acts: Luke 1:1-4; Acts 1:1; Acts 24:2; Luke 24:13-53; Acts 1:3-8

What Is the Gospel of Luke?

The Gospel of Luke is the first half of a larger work. The second half of it is the New Testament† book we know as The Acts of the Apostles. Neither half of the work can be easily or fully understood apart from the other half. We will find it useful, therefore, to make some use of Acts, even though the center of our attention will be on Luke. Scholars often use the term Luke-Acts* to refer to the complete work.

The scope of Luke (volume I of Luke-Acts) is limited to the story of the earthly life of Jesus. It begins with events preparing for his birth and ends with his resurrection appearances. Acts (volume II) picks up where Luke ends and tells of the beginning of the church in Jerusalem and its expansion into the Hellenistic-Roman world. It ends with the preaching of Paul in the capital city of the empire— Rome itself.

---

*Words with an asterick can be found in the glossary at the back of the book.

---

†I use the traditional terms "Old Testament" and "New Testament" with some serious misgivings.

Especially since Jewish experience of the Holocaust in Hitler's Germany, we Christians have been forced to reexamine the implicit anti-semitic factors in our religion as a whole. The traditional designations of the two parts of our Bible as "Old" and "New" tends to reflect unfavorably on the first as inferior to the second. This implication is contrary to Christian orthodoxy, which affirms the full inspiration of the whole Bible.

At present, no alternative terminology seems better. André Lacocque

1

Why Was It Written?

In the preface to Luke (Luke 1:1-4), the author said that his purpose was to write an orderly and accurate account of the origin and early years of the Christian movement. He acknowledged some indebtedness to earlier accounts, and to eyewitnesses, and to ministers of the word. Also he reported that his study of these matters had been "for some time now." He stated that a primary purpose was to inform a person addressed as "most excellent Theophilos."* Either Theophilos was the name of a person otherwise unknown or a general term for any "friend of God." The presence of an honorific title makes it more likely that "Theophilos" was the name of a person in high public office, a Roman official like "most excellent Felix" of Acts 24:2.

Since the book was addressed to Theophilos, Luke placed special emphasis on the good relationship that the early Christian leaders had with Roman officials. Perhaps the emphasis was to inform Theophilos that the Romans who knew Jesus and Paul were friendly and supportive. At the most significant point, the execution of Jesus by the Romans, Luke reported that Pilate declared him innocent, three times, in fact, and placed the blame on the Jews. Some scholars guess that Roman persecution had already begun and that Luke's Gospel was defending the innocence of Christians.

But Luke also had another purpose: to add to the story a new body of teachings of Jesus. Many of the teachings, such as the Parable of the Prodigal Son (15:11-32) or the Parable of the Good Samaritan (Luke 10:33-37), are preserved only in Luke.

---

has proposed that we call the older part the "Prime Testament" (in *Biblical Studies*, L. Boadt, H. Cooner, and L. Klenicke, editors, p. 121). But that's "reverse discrimination" because "Prime" cannot be taken as the designation for the "Old Testament" without carrying with it implications of superiority. Paul van Buren has proposed "Hebrew Scriptures" for the Old Testament and "Apostolic Writings" for the New, but the Old Testament is partly in Aramaic, and "Scriptures" implies superiority over "Writings." "Hebrew" and "Greek" scriptures is closer to a good solution, but the needed new way has not yet emerged.

I will therefore, reluctantly, continue to use the traditional designation.

Still another purpose of Luke is closely related. His research led him to believe that some earlier writers were mistaken about some important points. He expanded their story and also corrected parts of it. All these earlier accounts ("many" according to Luke 1:1) have been lost, except one. Most scholars believe our Gospel of Mark was one of the earlier accounts. If this is true, then we can compare Mark with Luke and discover the parts of Mark that Luke believed were mistaken and therefore corrected. For example, Mark looks ahead to an appearance of the Risen Lord to the eleven disciples in Galilee (Mark 14:28 and 16:7), but in Luke the appearances are restricted to Jerusalem and Emmaus (Luke 24:49 and Acts 1:4). These differences help us understand the individual viewpoint of each of these Gospels and help clarify our understanding of the purposes of Luke.

When Was It Written?

Luke is not dated. Scholars usually guess that it was written late in the first Christian century, some time after Mark. Mark was written about the year 70 according to ancient tradition and modern scholarship. Scholarly guesses range from late in the first century to early in the second. The writer of Luke was not an eyewitness but belonged to the second generation of Christians according to the preface of the Gospel.

Who Wrote It?

Like all the other canonical Gospels, the third one is anonymous. Tradition has assigned the authorship to "Luke," who is mentioned as a companion of Paul in Colossians 4:14 and described in 2 Timothy 4:11 as the only one who remained with him to the end. In Colossians, Luke is called "the beloved physician." This tradition of authorship first appeared in a work of Irenaeus* around 185 C.E. (Common Era).*

3

This tradition has been accepted during most of the history of the church. Now, however, scholarship is divided about the accuracy of this tradition, largely because of serious discrepancies between Acts and Paul's major letters, Romans, Corinthians, and Galatians. If the physician Luke, companion of Paul, did not write it, we don't know who did. In this study we shall not argue for one side or the other of this quarrel; but, for convenience, we will continue to use the traditional name Luke to refer to the author.

Since Luke is written in excellent idiomatic Greek, rivaling the Epistle to the Hebrews as the best in the New Testament, it seems justified to assume that its author was well educated and belonged to the cultured upper classes. We might also assume that Luke was a converted Gentile, probably a Greek, rather than a Roman. Many Hellenistic Jews,* however, were fluent in literary Greek, so Luke may have been one of them. We cannot infer much about his cultural identity from his name; the Apostle Paul, for instance, was a Hellenistic Jew with the Roman name "Paulus."

The religious viewpoint expressed in Luke (see below) indicates that the author, whether a converted Gentile or a Hellenistic Jew, was quite "conservative" in his outlook. "Conservative" in the first century meant "more Jewish than Gentile." Luke was not nearly as "liberal" as Paul and did not share Paul's sense of freedom from the Law.

How Was It Written?

The author's preface (Luke 1:1-4) tells us that Luke was written after consulting the earlier written accounts, the traditions that came from the eyewitnesses, and the ministers of the word (early Christian preachers). He studied these sources "for some time past" (1:3) and then put the story in the order he believed was right, using his own judgment of what was accurate. He used research procedures familiar to us, under the inspiration of the Holy

4

Spirit, to produce his great two-volume work Luke-Acts.

Scholars have identified one of his principal sources as our Gospel of Mark, which was used also by the author of the Gospel of Matthew. Luke used Mark carefully, shortened some of the stories, and rewrote parts to improve the literary quality. To see both of these traits, compare Mark 5:21-43 with Luke 8:40-56. Luke also omitted parts of Mark. Luke quoted his sources accurately but sometimes added an explanation or comment that gives the reader a different impression. To see these traits, compare Mark 14:32-42 with Luke 22:39-46.

What Is Its Viewpoint?

Luke understood Christianity as the true form of the old religion; Christianity was the true Israel. The Gospel of Luke reveals that its author was loyal to the central tenets of Judaism. He knew the Hebrew scriptures well (but in their Greek translation). He began his Gospel with the scene of Zechariah in the Temple and ended it with the post-resurrection note that the followers of Jesus were "continually in the Temple, praising God." He treated Jerusalem with special veneration. Unlike the authors of Mark and Matthew, Luke took special pains to confine the resurrection appearances to the Holy City or nearby Emmaus. It was in Jerusalem that the church was born, with the coming of the Holy Spirit at Pentecost. According to Luke-Acts, the law of Moses was authoritative for Jesus (Luke 16:17), for Paul (Acts 21:24), and for Christianity in general.

Luke showed a special concern for the traditional forms of Jewish piety—prayer, fasting, and almsgiving. He had a decidedly Jewish view of the Holy Spirit (like that in the Hebrew scriptures). He also understood the powers of a healer in a specifically Jewish sense. (See pp. 54-56.)

Luke assumed a Jewish view of the oneness of the human body. Body, mind, and soul (spirit) are all aspects of a unity and are thoroughly interrelated. (See pp. 17-20.)

5

What Is Its Structure?

Following is an outline of the organization of Luke:

Chapter	Subject
1:1—2:52	Birth Stories of John and Jesus
3:1—4:13	Jesus' Baptism, Temptations The Beginnings of his Ministry
4:14—9:50 9:51—19:27	The Journey to Jerusalem Luke's Special Section
19:28—23:56	The Passion Week
24:1-53	The Empty Tomb Resurrection Appearances

What Are Its Additional Concerns?

Luke showed a special interest in several topics. He mentioned prayer more frequently than the other Evangelists and emphasized the role of the Holy Spirit. Many scholars think Luke's emphasis on the Holy Spirit was intended to convince both Theophilos and his Christian readers that Christianity—the true Israel—was not a human movement but a divinely founded and guided religion.

He also gave a special place to the role of women in the life of Jesus and in the earliest history of the church.

Luke showed special interest in the ministry of healing. In the Gospel, he characteristically united the ministry of the word in preaching and teaching and the ministry of service to all the needs of human beings. Luke gave special emphasis to the holistic nature of Jesus' ministry and that of the apostolic church.

These special interests are in addition to Luke's main

purposes. Each of the main purposes and each of the special interests are excellent subjects for intensive study.

The Focus of This Study

This study-book has a definite focus. It does not attempt to study all the aspects of the Gospel of Luke. It does not even select the main purposes. Instead, it gives specialized attention to the holistic nature of Jesus' ministry and focuses on his concern for the healing of persons. We will note all the healing stories in Luke and relate these stories to the ministry of the church today. Following is a list of these stories and the chapter(s) in which they will be discussed in this book. Two references, however, are too general in nature to be helpful in this study (Nos. 20 and 21 in the list below).

The Healing Stories in Luke

Story	Luke	Text Chapter
1. Man with unclean demon	4:33-37	6, 10
2. Peter's mother-in-law	4:38-39	6, 10
3. Sick with various diseases	4:40-41	4
4. A leper	5:12-14	4, 5, 10
5. Multitudes	5:15-16	2, 4, 5, 10
6. Paralyzed man	5:17-26	6, 7, 8, 10
7. Man's withered hand	6:6-11	6, 10
8. Multitudes	6:17-19	4, 7, 8
9. Centurion's servant	7:1-10	2, 3, 6, 10
10. Widow's son	7:11-17	4, 10
11. Multitudes	7:18-23	10
12. Woman of the city	7:36-50	3
13. Gerasene demoniac	8:26-39	6, 7, 8, 10
14. Jairus' daughter	8:40-42, 49-56	4, 6, 10
15. Woman with flow of blood	8:43-48	3, 4, 7, 10
16. Multitudes	9:10-11	2, 7, 10
17. Child with convulsive spirit	9:37-43	5, 6, 7, 8
18. Man with a dumb demon	11:14-25	7, 8
19. Woman with spirit of infirmity	13:10-17	4, 6, 7, 10
20. Various persons	13:31-35	
21. Man with dropsy	14:1-6	
22. Ten lepers	17:11-18	7
23. Blind beggar	18:35-43	3, 6, 10
24. Slave's ear	22:47-53	4, 8

2 The Unity of Religion and Health

Readings from Luke: 4:16-21; 5:15; 9:1-2, 6, 11; 10:9, 29-37

Jesus' Holistic Ministry

Early in his ministry, Jesus returned to "Nazareth, where he had been brought up," entered the synagogue on the sabbath, and "stood up to read" (4:16). He was handed the Isaiah scroll. He turned the scroll until he came to the passage we have numbered as Isaiah 61:1-2. It is the great passage where the unknown prophet of post-exilic times announced that "the Spirit of the Lord" was upon him, anointing him (a Messianic phrase) to preach "good news" (another way of translating the Greek word for "gospel") to the poor.

The word "messiah" means "the anointed one." In Israel's national era 1020-586 B.C.E. (Before Common Era),* the king, who was anointed with oil by a religious authority, was regarded as "the anointed one" (Messiah). After the national era, there were no more kings. For a brief period in the last part of the second century B.C.E. and the first part of the first century B.C.E., the Jews in the Jerusalem area were independent and had their own Priest-King. After that, some Roman-appointed rulers, like Herod the Great, were given kingly status, but these kings were Roman agents.

Jews living under oppressive foreign rulers (Assyrians, Babylonians, Persians, Greeks, and Romans in that order) began to hope for, and believe in, a coming king who would restore their fortunes as a people. Thus arose "the Messianic hope" among the Jews. This development is fully explained in J. Klausner, *The Messianic Hope in Israel* (1955), and in S. Mowinckel, *He that Cometh* (1954).

9

Jesus claimed for himself this Isaiah passage with its reference to being anointed by the Spirit of the Lord. In this conception, however, the anointed one was not to be a ruling king but a proclaimer of the gospel ("good news") of God's concern for the poor, the captives, the blind, and the oppressed.

> "The Spirit of the Lord is upon me,
> because he has anointed me to preach good news to the poor.
> He has sent me to proclaim release to the captives
> and recovering of sight to the blind,
> to set at liberty those who are oppressed,
> to proclaim the acceptable year of the Lord." (4:18-19)

In applying this prophecy to himself, Jesus was announcing that his was not merely a preaching ministry. He was also anointed to heal and to bring release and freedom to the captives and the oppressed. This is a classic statement of a holistic view of ministry.

Luke had prepared the reader for this in the infancy stories. In the "Magnificat" of Mary (1:46-55), especially in verses 51-53, the holistic nature of Jesus' coming ministry is clearly predicted.

True to these declarations from Mary before Jesus was born and from Jesus at the very beginning of his ministry, Luke described the ministry of Jesus as fulfilling these bold claims. The people came to see Jesus—"to hear and to be healed" (5:15). When Jesus sent the Twelve on their mission, he sent them "to preach the Kingdom of God and to heal" (9:2). They received Jesus' instructions, and "went through the villages, preaching the gospel and healing everywhere" (9:6). When the Twelve returned, Jesus withdrew with them to Bethsaida, but the people discovered him. Jesus welcomed them and "spoke to them of the Kingdom of God and cured those who had need of healing" (9:11). Later, Jesus appointed seventy others and sent them out in teams of two. They were instructed to enter a town, "heal the sick in it and say to them 'the Kingdom of God has come near you'" (10:9).

Luke is the only Gospel that contains the Parable of the

Good Samaritan (10:29-37). This parable clearly teaches that discipleship is just as concerned with ministry to physical needs as it is with a spiritual witness.

We can see from Luke that religion and health went together in Luke's understanding of the ministry of Jesus. Jesus, the Great Evangelist, was also Jesus, the Great Physician. For the Christian, this is the the primary healing tradition from antiquity, the standard by which we should shape our practices today.

The Unity of Greek Medicine

In actual Christian history, another ancient healing tradition, the Greek, has been more influential than the Jewish tradition that Jesus exemplified. The Greek healing tradition has one of its roots in the mythology of Asklepios, the Greek healing-god. His cult gained popularity during the fourth century B.C.E. and spread to Rome early in the next century, where he was known as Aesculapius. In the earliest period of Christian history, Asklepios "was regarded by early Christians as the chief competitor of Christ because of his remarkable similarity in role and teachings to the Great Physician."[1] Shrines (sanctuaries) dedicated to Asklepios became famous healing centers all over the Hellenistic world. These were the principal hospitals of antiquity.

Like the Jewish healing tradition exemplified in Jesus, this Greek medical tradition treated the whole person, not just the physical aspect. This is evident in the operation of a sanitarium of Asklepios, such as the famous one at Epidauros or the one in Pergamum.

Cures had to be initiated by Asklepios who called the sick person to the healing center. This call was usually indicated by the appearance of a serpent (the chief symbol of Asklepios) in a dream. Upon arrival, the one desiring to be

[1]Darrel W. Amundsen and Gary B. Ferngren, *Health/Medicine and the Faith Traditions*, ed. Marty and Vaux (Philadelphia: Fortress Press, 1982), p. 80.

11

healed first went through a period of inner reflection, ridding himself or herself of all personal animosities toward others, confessing all wrongs, and removing guilt feelings. This was their method of purifying the mind and spirit. Then one waited for the summons into the sanctuary. This summons, like the initial call, was usually signified by the appearance of a serpent in a dream. When the priests were persuaded that the "patient" was invited into the sanctuary, he or she spent the night there, hoping for a sign of the god's presence and healing powers.

Many persons reported cures; many were not cured. Those who were cured usually left a votive tablet in the shrine recording their name, their ailment, and their cure. Excavators of these shrines have found hundreds of votive tablets.[2] All people who made the journey, whether cured or not, found the pilgrimage to be beneficial for their lives as a whole.

The impact of the Asklepios-tradition upon Christian civilization was deep and permanent. His symbol, the snake twined around a staff, is the standard symbol of the physician (Jewish and Christian alike). His two daughters, Panacea (cure-all) and Hygieia (health; hygiene) have become household words.

The Asklepian tradition of sleeping in sacred precincts (the *abaton*) to be healed is technically called "incubation."* Its roots go back to earlier Egyptian religion where ill persons slept in the tomb of Imhotep, Egypt's healing god. Even while Christianity was triumphing over this ancient religion, "incubation temples" remained popular throughout the Greco-Roman world. In fact, the custom was never abolished but "Christianized" and practiced in Christian churches. "In the Middle Ages, for instance, churches were sometimes equipped with mattresses and even baths for this purpose, a church in Cambridge [England] being particularly renowned for its incubation cures: and the practice is not yet extinct in the Greek Orthodox persuasion

---

[2]Many of these are transcribed and translated in Dr. Edgar J. Swift, *Jungle of the Mind*. Facsimile edition of 1931 publication. Essay Index Reprint.

12

and in certain corners of Roman Catholicism."[3]

In these earlier pre-modern days, both in the Asklepian Greek tradition and in medieval Christianity, "when medicine was bound up with religious ideas there was nothing to prevent the physician considering his patient [or the priest considering his parishioner] as a whole person."[4]

By way of contrast, the Hebrew tradition perceived the unity of religion and health apart from the priesthood. "There appears to be no evidence for priests functioning as physicians..." in the Hebrew scriptures.[5] Instead, the "healing" work of the priesthood is connected with the belief that illness is punishment for sin and cured by sacrificial rituals. (See the chapter on "The Role of Malady.") Spiritual healing is associated with the prophets (especially Elijah and Elisha), not with the priests. Jesus was a part of the prophet-healer tradition of Judaism.

Early Christian Traditions

Christianity arose in an atmosphere that was generally hostile. Suffering was accepted—almost expected—by many Christians. Because of the persecutions, strength to bear suffering was needed more than the healing emphasis characteristic of earlier apostolic times. (See the chapters on "The Role of Malady" and "Technique or Grace?")

After the persecutions were over, a late fourth century church leader Basil the Great wrote a tract on why Christians were still afflicted with illness. He listed six reasons. Illness, he wrote, might be:

1. sent by God as discipline to develop character.

2. sent by God as punishment for sin.

3. given to those God knows are strong enough to bear it as models for the weak.

4. sent to check one's sense of self-importance.

---

[3]Louis Rose, *Faith Healing*, revised from 1968 Gollancz edition (New York: Penguin Books, 1971), p. 25.

[4]Rose, p. 18.

[5]Darrell W. Amundsen and Gary B. Ferngren in Marty and Vaux, p. 65.

5. an affliction sent by Satan.

6. simply the result of poor nutrition or some similar natural cause.

Basil recommended consulting a physician when the illness was sent by God as discipline or when it was the result of natural causes. He made no recommendation for the other four causes.

The pattern illustrated in Basil is characteristic for most of the remainder of church history. When illness occurred:

> Some Christians relied exclusively on prayer, others combined secular medicine with prayer. Some resorted to secular medicine only when prayer proved ineffective, while others turned to prayer only when secular medicine did not avail. Some sought a more dramatic approach to divine intervention than prayer (e.g. faith healing, involving a variety of procedures) and had no recourse to physicians. Others sought such religious means only as a last resort after physicians have despaired. These different attitudes still exist side by side within Christianity and cults peripheral to it.[6]

The early church's recognition of "secular medicine" marked the beginnings of a separation between medicine and religion. Spiritual healing was on the decline in the mainstream of Christianity, and "secular medicine" was recognized as independent of the church.

Several practices developed in the Middle Ages which contributed to the decline of earlier forms of spiritual healing. Among these was an increasingly popular appeal to the saints for healing and especially to the curative powers of their relics. Sacramental healing gradually transformed the practice of "unction" (anointing the sick with oil to restore health as directed in James 5:14-15) into the Sacrament of Extreme Unction (anointing the dying for the salvation of their souls). The church also increasingly related the "mentally ill" to demon-possession.

The Loss of Holism in Protestantism

Protestant leaders, in their protests over non-scriptural

---

[6]Amundsen and Ferngren, p. 101.

Catholic practices, rejected relic-veneration healing, rejected the Sacrament of Extreme Unction, and pushed exorcism
to the fringes of the church. John Calvin, for example,

> viewed medieval healing practices with disdain, ironically
> mocking the use of relics. Further, he held that the age of
> miracles was past, including healing by non-physical means,
> except by divine action. Calvin's more "modern" attitude
> toward health became a part of the tradition associated with his
> name [the Reformed Tradition].... Illness... was still often
> considered to be divine punishment or testing....[7]

These attitudes contributed to the separation of religion
and physical health that is typical in modern Christianity.
Most Christians today have driven a wedge between
religion and health. Very few of us would consult our pastor
about our health problems. Nor would we take our religious
questions or problems to our local physician. The pastor's
business is spiritual matters; the physician's is physical or
mental health matters. In the words of Paul Tillich:
"Theology and medicine lost the intimate connection they
originally had, and always should have—for saving the
person is healing him."[8]

Although it is generally true that this intimate connection
has been lost, there are exceptions. We do have physicians
and ministers who are consciously striving to be holistic in
their practice. One conspicuous example of this is the
Hospice Movement, which provides physical, psychological, social, and spiritual care for the ill. Other examples
include the various holistic health associations and organi-
zations like the Society of Teachers of Family Medicine.
Nevertheless, a more specialized approach is still the
prevailing one.

The root of this unfortunate separation lies in the rise of
modern scientific medicine. This, in turn, roots back into

---

[7]James N. Lapsley, *Salvation and Health: The Interlocking Process of Life*
(Philadelphia: Westminster, 1972), pp. 41-42.

[8]"The Impact of Psychotherapy on Theological Thought," *The Churches'
Handbook for Spiritual Healing*, as cited by Lawrence W. Althouse in
Rediscovering the Gift of Healing (Nashville: Abingdon, 1977), p. 50.

another tradition of Greek medicine, one associated with the name Hippocrates rather than Asklepios. Hippocrates, in the fifth century B.C.E. rebelled at the religious and priestly elements in the Asklepios cult. By treating health problems as almost exclusively physical, rooted in nature rather than in a divinity, he earned and deserves the title of "the father of (modern) medicine." He pioneered the unfortunate breakdown of the earlier holistic approach characteristic of the Asklepian hospitals of antiquity.

The Asklepian tradition was endorsed by Plato, the Hippocratic tradition by Aristotle. It seems that modern medicine has emphasized the tradition of Hippocrates while ignoring the history of healing recorded on the votive tablets of the temples of Asklepios. Plato complained that the greatest error of his day was the separation of the concept of the soul from that of the body in medical treatment.[9] Modern medicine and modern Christian ministry alike need to hear this complaint again.

The Recovery of Unity

We are now beginning to recover the more ancient awareness of the essential unity of the human person. We are indebted both to the Hebrew and the Greek traditions of healing in this rediscovery and its meaning.

One form of the modern recovery is found in psychosomatic medicine. This field of research and practice is named after two Greek words, *soma* (body) and *psyche* (the soul-mind-spirit-emotions complex). It recognizes the interrelations of the "physical" and the "non-physical" aspects of a human being. It is discovering that the "physical" is not merely physical, and that the "non-physical" is not merely non-physical. These two aspects are so integrated that mental health, spiritual health, emotional health, and physical health are all interrelated. When any one of these aspects of humanity is ill, that illness affects all the others.

But even psychosomatic medicine has paid more atten-

---

[9]Rose, p. 20.

tion to the mental and emotional aspects of the "non-physical" than to the spiritual. Recent attention to spiritual health is helping to make that correction.

Healing illness in full cooperation with physicians is also a major function of the church. Jesus Christ did not come to save souls only, or to save bodies only, but to save people.

Another form of modern recovery has developed out of the powerful impact of Mary Baker Eddy and Christian Science. She perceived the closest kind of unity between the body and the spirit (soul-mind). All healing, for all aspects of a human being, was under spiritual control, according to her. Spiritual healing, however, was the only recognized kind. Medical physicians were displaced by "practitioners."

Eddy claimed that bodily ailments have a spiritual cause. In many instances, this has been verified. She went further than most Christians have followed when she claimed that *all* physical illness is rooted in spiritual disorder. The truth in what she taught has helped to awaken a new sensitivity to the interrelations between body and spirit. In the words of the Christian Scientist Robert Peel: "The urgent need of our time is for a coherent view of life, at the same time religious and scientific...."[10]

In spite of its insight and its sensitizing value, Christian Science fails to convince most practicing Christians because they feel it claims too much. In the last analysis, Christian Science doesn't hold the body and spirit together in unity. It raises the spirit to the level of the only reality and ultimately denies the reality of the whole physical world, including our bodies.

The Wholeness of Life

To live by a concept of the wholeness of life is very difficult for most of us. William E. Phipps has observed that, "Until the psychosomatic integration of Jesus' personality is recognized, there is little hope for the recovery of holism by

---

[10]*Moving Mountains* (British Broadcasting Corporation, 1956), p. 4.

those who worship him and who think they should pattern their lives after his." He goes on to note that "Christians will probably be unable to deal wholesomely with their own human nature. They will either actively deny their bodily needs, or not fully integrate their beliefs with their real lives."[11]

Sam Keen has recently argued quite convincingly for what he calls "a resurrection of the bodily" in the spiritually dominant environment of the church. He notes that "Incarnation, if it is anything more than a once-upon-a-time story, means grace is carnal, healing is through the flesh." He adds that "the sacred must be rediscovered in what moves and touches us, in what makes us tremble...."[12] Our bodies and our souls are inseparable aspects of the whole person.

In the Hebrew tradition, a human being was a living *nephesh*—a body-soul unity. When his or her relationship to God was right, that person was in *shalom** (health-wholeness-peace). In the early Christian Greek tradition, that right relationship was called *soteria** (salvation). We can see the Greek verb *sōzō* (the active aspect of the concept *soteria*) in its wider meaning in Luke 7:1-10. In verse three, the centurion asked Jesus to *diasōzē* (heal) his slave. He was not thinking about the spiritual condition of the slave but about his physical state. At the end of the story, in verse 10, the centurion returned to his house and found the slave *hygiainonta* (restored to health). *Sōzō* and *soteria* are here intimately linked with *hygiainō* (hygiene). Salvation means good health. *Shalom* and *soteria* include all dimensions of existences—the spiritual and physical, the individual and societal.

When one reflects on how this should affect the church's work in the world today, it is clear that our practice and our theology do not give much attention to the physical healing of persons and of society. Indeed, when the subject is raised

---

[11]*Recovering Biblical Sensuousness* (Philadelphia: Westminster, 1975), p. 158.
[12]Phipps, p. 158.

and human physical needs are brought up to the level of consciousness, we tend to get very uncomfortable and retreat into that dualism that leaves all of the individual physical health concerns to the physicians and the physical ills of society to the politicians, reserving for the church only spiritual health needs.

This attitude is especially typical of mainline Protestantism. Even in sectarian Protestantism, where the spiritual healing of personal physical ailments has remained a major concern of the Christian religion, there is often little or no awareness of the church's mission to society's illnesses. Personal physical healing by spiritual means tends to be "out-of-balance" with the rest of the Gospel. By the same standard, there is a sense in which mainline Protestantism has been off balance through its lack of attention to its role in physical health, both for the individual and society.

Through counseling and pastoral care, the churches have, in this century, done something to restore the fullness of the Gospel. But the inclusion of special attention to mental health problems is still very limited in most churches. If we fail to develop this more fully, then, as Howard Clinebell observes, "Mental health centers would then become the *de facto* churches in that they would be doing more to meet the growth and healing needs of persons than the churches."[13]

The churches are even more guilty when physical health problems are added to the concerns of the Christian mission. We refer most mental health problems and all physical health problems to specialists in those areas.

The wholeness which is broken by this specialization of spiritual and physical is illustrated by the etymology* of our English word "health." It comes from the Saxon word *hal*. From this root word, we have developed our word "hale," an almost obsolete word now surviving only in the popular phrase "hale and hearty," meaning in good health. From the same root comes our word "whole" and the commonest

---

[13]Howard Clinebell, ed., "Introduction," *Community Mental Health* (Nashville: Abingdon Press, 1970), p. 14.

greeting word "hello." Like *shalom*, "hello" is an expression wishing health and wholeness. Health and wholeness are thus etymologically bound together.

A recent study by Joseph H. Fichter investigates the spiritual dimension of health care. It asks the question, "Does modern medical practice take seriously the holistic approach to illness, which includes the spiritual as well as the physical, psychological, and social aspects of the human personality?" The "basic assumption" of the study is that "religion and spirituality are formally integrated with medicine and nursing not only in the... church-related hospitals but also in the pastoral-care departments" of non-church-related ones as well.[14]

"Formally" integrated, however, is not necessarily *practically* integrated. There is much to be done to bring about this needed integration.

We also need to broaden our definition of illness to include non-physical illnesses which do not seem to have an obvious effect on bodily health. They *do*, in fact, have an effect, and often a powerful one, but the connection often passes unnoticed:

> We are all handicapped, but some of us are handicapped in more immediately obvious ways. Who is to say, however, that a person twisted by an inability to love is less handicapped than someone crippled by polio? Who can say that someone blinded by jealousy is less handicapped than someone who has been physically blind from birth?[15]

One of the simplest and yet most effective ways of raising a congregation's level of consciousness of the unity of the mind-soul-spirit-emotions-body complex is through carefully planned worship experiences that exemplify this integration. Thomas and Sharon Neufer Emswiler have many helpful suggestions for doing this in their book *Wholeness in Worship*.

---

[14]*Religion and Pain: The Spiritual Dimension of Health Care* (New York: Crossroad, 1981), pp. 11-12.

[15]Thomas and Sharon Neufer Emswiler, *Wholeness in Worship* (New York: Harper and Row, 1980), p. 46.

3 The Role of Faith

Readings from Luke: 7:1-10, 36-50; 8:43-48; 17:5-6; 18:35-43

The Healings of Jesus

In two famous healing stories found only in Luke, Jesus stressed the role of faith as the key to the healing. Two others shared with Matthew and Mark make the same emphasis. In the first of these four, Jesus heals the slave of a centurion by a word spoken *in absentia* and then gives the centurion higher praise for his faith than any of those "in Israel." This is only an implicit affirmation of the role of faith in the healings of Jesus, but it seems justifiable to include it as an example of faith.

> In your opinion, what place does faith play in the healings done by (or through) Jesus?

The second story, also unique to Luke, contains Jesus' famous pronouncement to the woman of the city, "your faith has saved you; go in peace" (7:50). This story also involves the role of sin and repentance, which we'll examine in the chapter "The Role of Malady." The related stories in Mark 14:3-9, Matthew 26:6-13, and John 12:1-8 all make quite a different point and do not mention a faith dimension at all.

The same message, in exactly the same words (in Greek), appears in the story of the woman with the flow of blood

21

(Luke 8:43-48). This story is found also in Mark (Luke's probable source) and in Matthew. In Mark, the phrase is slightly different in the Greek text, though the Revised Standard Version obscures this difference by giving the English version an identity not present in the Greek. Mark's text says "your faith has saved you; go your way in peace" (Mark 5:34). Matthew has only "your faith has saved you" (Matthew 9:22).

In the story of the healing of the blind beggar at Jericho, Jesus says again "your faith has saved you" (Luke 18:42). His probable source Mark, who says the beggar's name is Bartimaeus, uses the same words, prefaced by, "Go your way" (Mark 10:52). This is the same preface-phrase that Mark used earlier in 5:34. Matthew not only replaces Bartimaeus by two blind men but also makes the healing effective by the touch of Jesus, leaving out the faith statement altogether (Matthew 20:29-34).

The key phrase, then, is reported three times in Luke, twice in Mark, and only once in Matthew. In all the quotations above, I have translated the Greek phrase literally "your faith has *saved* you." The Revised Standard Version translates it literally only once (in Luke 7:50). In all the others, it is translated "your faith has *made you well*." This is a legitimate option, because the verb (*sōzō*) has both meanings: it usually means to save or rescue or deliver from some danger and therefore was used also to mean to heal or to cure. The word itself, as shown above on p. 18, illustrates the unity of religion and health.

How do the two translations ("saved" or "made well") illustrate the unity of religion and health?

Luke reports 24 episodes about Jesus' healing activities. Faith is lifted up as important only in these four. Of course, it can be assumed to be present in many others, perhaps in most of them. But one could also assume that Jesus healed by touch even when the touching is not mentioned, and so

> How significant is it to you that only one-sixth of the
> healing reports in Luke specifically mention faith? ✓

on for each factor. That faith is an important element is
beyond question. But just *how* important is it?

The term "faith-healing" puts an exaggerated emphasis
on the role of faith in healing. Typical of many of those
deeply involved in the healing ministry of the church,
Francis MacNutt begins his discussion on "The Faith to Be
Healed" with the too-strong statement: "All the books on
healing—including *the* book on healing, the New Testament—emphasize the role that faith plays in healing. 'Go in
peace, your faith has made you whole,' is a constant saying
of Jesus."[1] I have no quarrel with the translation "whole,"
rather than "made well" or "saved," because the verb
means all those things. But, since this pronouncement of
Jesus occurs in only three stories, and exactly like that in
only two of them, it is hardly justifiable to describe it as "a
constant saying of Jesus." Let's acknowledge, then, that, in
one-sixth of the healing reports in Luke, Jesus heals in the
presence of explicit faith. In all the others, either different
factors are emphasized, or no factor is mentioned.

Whose Faith Is Needed?

In three of the faith-healings in Luke, it is the faith of the
healed person which activates the healing (and in one of
these, the account in another Gospel omits the faith
dimension: Matthew 20:29-34).

Another faith-healing calls special attention to the faith of
the centurion. He was neither the healer nor the one healed
but a "third party" (a general name for one who is neither
the healer nor the recipient). Is this story telling us that in
some way "third party faith" can be effective in healing?

---

[1]MacNutt, p. 99.

Do you believe that faith is essential on the part of persons who need to be healed? Why or why not?

Who needs to have faith—the healer or the one healed, or someone else? Any one of them? Is it more effective if all three are present? Are two better than one?

Although Luke has no healing stories that emphasize the role of the healer's faith, the larger evidence makes it mandatory to include this as another dimension. Luke does stress the power of faith in the teachings of Jesus. Once the disciples came to Jesus with the request that he "increase their faith" (17:5-6). Although he did not respond to their plea, he made a strong statement about the power of faith: a tiny amount (like a grain of mustard seed) is sufficient to uproot a sycamore tree and plant it in the sea. This refers to the power of faith in the healer, rather than the healed person, but it could apply also to the faith of the third party.

Perhaps a caution is in order here to help keep our thinking straight. We all tend to read factors into the data that we think should (or must) be there, even though unmentioned. When we do this, our pre-conceptions govern our use of the data. Werner Heisenberg, in his *Physics and Beyond*, reports that Albert Einstein once said to him: "It is the theory which decides what we can observe."[2] Mary Baker Eddy made a similar statement in her *Science and Health*. She said, "Mortal mind sees what it believes as certainly as it believes what it sees."[3] For example, if one is already convinced that faith on the part of the one who needs healing is an essential, then one will assume that faith in all instances of spiritual healing and explain all failures as

---

[2](New York: Harper and Row, 1971), p. 63.

The larger context of the quotation is "...It may be heuristically useful to keep in mind what one has actually observed. But on principle, it is quite wrong to try founding a theory on observable magnitudes alone. In reality the very opposite happens. It is the theory which decides what we can observe."

[3](Boston: The First Church, 1906), p. 86, lines 29-30.

due to a lack of faith. And so it goes with each other element in this mysterious realm.

Different Concepts of Faith

Whether on the part of the first party (the healer), the second party (the one who is healed) or the third party (anyone else), faith is commonly understood as trust, belief, confidence, and hope, combined in one powerful attitude. This faith can be in God's power to intervene in a special way, or in some "immutable laws" of God that govern health. (See the chapter "Technique or Grace.")

This faith is often augmented by "imaging" the final result. "Imaging" is more powerful than "imagining" the desired result. It is more like seeing the forthcoming results ahead of time. Just *how* imaging helps is not explained in the same ways by those who advocate it or those who have experienced its benefits. For some,[4] it is the calling out of the powers of the subconscious mind, with its link to Infinite Power. With others it is a kind of psychic pre-cognition, partly, but not wholly, involving the human will. For still others it is one way to create and maintain a positive attitude that in itself is a factor in the healing process.

Do you know of an example in your own experience of someone who has been helped by "imaging" the final result?

Others experience faith as a close and intimate relationship with God (or Christ or the Holy Spirit). This is a relationship of acceptance (God's acceptance of us) and inner transformation, freely given to unworthy persons. It is the kind of faith that many believe Paul was trying to proclaim—faith as a gift of God—a newly-given acceptance

---

[4]Joseph Murphy, *The Power of Your Subconscious Mind* (1963; rpt. Englewood Cliffs, New Jersey: Prentice-Hall, 1981), p. 76.

of sinners and an indwelling spirit to transform the sinner into the image of Christ.

For many persons "faith" means "*the* faith." It means having the correct doctrines. John Sanford describes this faith as "... a total acceptance of a religious system.... The person who is able to accept all that is offered to him with little or no doubt, is a faithful member."[5]

It is easy to confuse faith with optimism. Paul Tournier reflects on his own experience with this tendency:

> I am by nature optimistic, whereas my wife is pessimistic. I am confident, she is apprehensive. For a long time I reproached her for her pessimism as indicating a lack of faith. For my own part I prided myself on my optimistic outlook as if it came from my faith and not from my inborn disposition. One day, when we both had a great act of faith to perform, I realized during my quiet time that I was being less than honest in confusing faith with optimism, to my own advantage. The truth was that real faith was as difficult for me as it was for my wife.[6]

Another way to approach the meaning of faith is to look at its opposite, "fear." "Fear," Robert Leslie observes:

> is probably the most common and subtle of diseases. Fear can affect virtually every organ of the body.... Fear invites illness.... *Faith is the opposite of fear*. Faith has a transforming and healing power that literally achieves miracles. When cures of serious organic diseases occur without medical intervention, researchers often find that strong faith has been at work.[7]

He notes that one can describe the whole ministry of Jesus as one of deliverance from fear. "Do not be afraid" is a phrase Jesus used frequently. "Jesus' answer for fear was always the same," Leslie maintains, "Fear is overcome by faith..."[8] (2 Timothy 1:7).

---

[5]John Sanford, *Healing and Wholeness* (New York: Paulist Press, 1977), p. 11.

[6]Paul Tournier, *The Healing of Persons*, translated by Edwin Hudson (New York: Harper and Row, 1965), pp. 79-80.

[7]Robert Leslie, *Health, Healing and Holiness* (Nashville: Graded Press, 1971), p. 39.

[8]Leslie, p. 39.

> Can you give examples of how fears are overcome by faith?

Is Faith Essential?

The role that faith plays in health is clearly positive, but is it essential? If so, what *kind* of faith is essential?

Contrary to common assumptions, faith on the part of the ill person cannot be regarded as essential. No one doubts its beneficial values, but an essential—a "without which not" (*sine qua non*)—it isn't. This is clearly demonstrated in those genuine healings where the one who is healed is not a person of faith. Atheists have been healed. Skeptics of the whole process of spiritual healings, including those who don't believe in the healer's healing powers, have been spiritually healed. When a man came to Mrs. Worrall for healing and first confessed that he was an atheist and had no faith, she told him not to worry; she had enough faith for both.[9]

Probably the most convincing reason for thinking that the faith of the healed person is not essential comes from the spiritual healing of animals and plants. (See pp. 33-34.) It is very difficult to attribute anything like faith—in any of the popular senses—to animals or plants.

Not only is faith on the part of the one who is healed not essential; neither is faith on the part of the healer. The faith of the third party is made non-essential by the many instances of healing where there is no third party.

But to recognize that faith is a non-essential to the whole process of spiritual healing is not to deny that faith is often a powerful factor. Faith can even be *the crucial factor* in some healings. Faith, in all of its meanings and in all three parties, is always a positive element in the healing process. But the

[9]Joyce Hopkins, "Miracle of Healing...," *United Methodist Reporter* (May 1, 1981), p. 3.

process is more mysterious than we can explain, at least at the present time. In the realistic summary of Francis MacNutt, Faith "is often—but not always—a precondition for healing."[10] Or again, "The faith needed for healing can be in anyone—or no one."[11]

Faith Is a Gift

Whether faith is trust or a personal relationship with God, it is important to emphasize again that "it is not our own doing; it is the gift of God" (Ephesians 2:8). Striving to achieve faith is a fruitless struggle. It reminds Francis MacNutt of:

> what often happens when I begin to lose a tennis game. I start overstraining; I hit the ball harder, trying to make winning shots in order to regain my confidence; I smash my serve harder to make a few quick, impressive aces. But all that really happens is that I hit the ball out of court more often, and I begin missing my first serve. My straining efforts worsen my game.... I only end up beating myself.[12]

He goes on, "...I am trying to create faith in myself, forgetting that faith is a gift from God."[13]

Again and again, the deeper answer of mainstream Christianity patiently explains how faith comes. It is not an achievement but a work of grace. We can put ourselves in the means of grace and then wait in patience while remaining active in our service to others in response to grace already achieved. (See the chapter "Technique or Grace?" for further explanations of "grace.")

---

[10]MacNutt, p. 105.
[11]MacNutt, p. 116.
[12]MacNutt, pp. 107-108.
[13]MacNutt, p. 109.

4 The Role of Touch

Readings from Luke: 4:40; 5:12-16; 6:17-19; 7:11-17; 8:40-56; 13:10-17; 22:47-53

How Jesus Used Touch

In Luke the ministry of Jesus clearly begins on the theme of Jesus' healing activity. After several specific healings described in chapter four, there is a general statement, "all those who had any that were sick with various diseases brought them to him" (4:40). Then the summary statement goes on to say that "he laid his hands on every one of them and healed them" (4:40).

Healing by "laying on of hands" is characteristic of Jesus, especially in Luke. Once when approached by a leper who asked to be healed, Jesus "stretched out his hand, and touched him" (5:13), telling him that he would be clean. The story reports that the leprosy left him "immediately" (5:13).

On another occasion, after spending an entire night in prayer, Jesus was the center of another multitude which had come from Judea and Jerusalem and the seacoast of Tyre and Sidon. He cured those who were demon-possessed, and then the account reports that "all the crowd sought to touch him, for power came forth from him and healed them all" (6:19).

One of the most amazing of the "touching stories" in Luke is the one that tells about Jesus encountering a procession carrying a dead man out of the city of Nain. It was accompanied by the dead man's mother, a widow. He was her only son. Jesus saw her weeping, "had compassion on her," and touched the bier carrying the dead man. The procession halted. Then Jesus told the young man to rise up and he did so, talking as he sat up (7:11-15). Here Jesus did not touch the man directly but only the bier.

Two stories are combined in another account. One story is begun only to be interrupted by another. Then the first one is completed. In both of them, touching is an important element. The first story tells of a dying girl, only twelve years old, who was restored to health when Jesus took her by the hand and told her to arise. The second is an even more dramatic instance of the power of touching. In it a woman who had "a flow of blood" for twelve years came through the crowd and touched "the fringe of his garment" and was immediately healed. Here the touch was indirectly made, rather than skin to skin.[1]

Another instance of Jesus healing by the "laying on of hands" is in the story of the bent over woman: "Now he was teaching in one of the synagogues on the sabbath. And there was a woman who had had a spirit of infirmity for eighteen years; she was bent over and could not fully straighten herself. And when Jesus saw her, he called her and said to her, "'Woman, you are freed from your infirmity'" (13:10-12). She could not stand up straight until Jesus laid his hands on her and "immediately she was made straight" (13:13).

When Jesus was arrested in the garden of Gethsemane, one of his disciples (identified as Peter in John 18:10) drew his sword and cut off the ear (the right ear in John) of the slave of the High Priest (identified as "Malchus" in John). Jesus immediately responded, "'No more of this!'" Then "he touched his ear and healed him" (22:51).

In every case except one, Jesus is described as using his hands to heal, healing by touching. In the other case, a woman seeking healing touched his garment.

Touching was by no means unique with Jesus. The Apostles healed by touch (Acts 19:11-12): "And God did extraordinary miracles by the hands of Paul, so that

---

[1]Note the interesting parallel in Acts 19:11-12. Note also that Matthew (9:18-26) associates the healing with Jesus' words rather than the woman's touch. In both accounts the woman's faith is lifted up as important.

handkerchiefs or aprons were carried away from his body to the sick, and diseases left them and the evil spirits came out of them." It was a common healing method in ancient times and has continued to be practiced ever since.

> What is the attitude toward healing by touch in your local church? What has contributed to this point of view?

Neither has it been limited to Mediterranean or European culture. Healing by touch is portrayed in cave drawings as early as 15,000 years ago and is mentioned in the earliest examples of writing. It is common in India, China, Tibet and elsewhere in the Orient. It is a universal process that is equally present in the healing activities of all cultures.

The Healer as Agent

Precisely how touching sometimes heals is still not known. In both the past and the present, it is often explained in terms of supernatural power expressing itself through the human healer. Since healing is usually viewed as "good," the supernatural power was regarded as "good" also. That is, a good god was the real healer. In Jewish experience, this power was "Yahveh." In Christian experience, it was Christ. In other religions, it was another supernatural power by another name.

For those Christians who are provincial in their own religion, the existence of healings by touch in non-Christian settings becomes a serious theological problem. Such Christians tend either to be skeptical of the reality of such healings or to assign them to Satan, as was done by Christians in the late Middle Ages in Europe and is done among some fundamentalists today,. Satan doing good? Yes, they say, but with a bad motive—namely, to lead away the faithful into heresy or apostasy.*

The traditional Christian explanation that it is Christ

31

healing through the touch of a human stems from the earliest traditions of Christianity. Acts reports both Peter (3:6) and Paul (16:18) healing "in the name of Jesus." Similarly a modern healer-by-touch, Oskar Estebany, a devout Roman Catholic from Hungary, "when pressed..., would say he felt he was a channel for the spirit of Jesus the Christ."[2]

Other modern Christian healers usually say the same thing. Well-known Protestant healers Olga Worrall of the New Life Clinic at Mt. Washington United Methodist Church in Baltimore, Maryland, and Agnes Sanford, who lives in California, agree. They illustrate the traditional "in house" explanation of the healing powers of touching. These Christian explanations are like those of other religions, each believing that its special way of grasping the reality of the divine presence is the secret of the healing touch.

Has your local church had a healing service? If so, what was it like?

A Modern Alternative

Contemporary research is moving in new directions. Most of it is very recent. All of it is in the present century. More research is needed before we can draw any sound conclusions. In the research data we now have, it does appear that touching itself is not the source of healing. The person who is doing the touching seems to be the clue to the healing powers of touching. The healer is the source of the healing touch. ("The Role of the Healer" will be discussed in a separate chapter.)

Controlled touching experiments demonstrate that the touch of certain persons is more effective in healing than

[2]Dolores Krieger, *The Therapeutic Touch* (Englewood Cliffs, New Jersey: Prentice-Hall, Inc, 1979), p. 6.

touches from randomly chosen persons. The experiments are most informative when the maladies are not in human subjects but in animals, or even plants. Oskar Estebany discovered his healing power when he was able to heal horses in the Austrian cavalry. People then brought their ill pets, and he healed some of these. Afterward he began to use his gift to benefit humans and has continued to help humans ever since.

Have you personally experienced healing through touch? in a religious setting? in another setting? Describe the healing.

Touch experiments that use animals or plants as subjects have certain advantages over those that use human subjects. Humans are endowed with imagination and preconceptions that may invalidate, or at least complicate, the experiment. Animals are not as subject to suggestion and can be presumed to have no expectations that might affect the results. Plants are even more "objective" subjects.

Currently, most healers are reluctant to "waste" their powers on animals or plants when humans are in need. In addition, while many healers are dedicated and devoted to their work, they may not be scientifically minded and may not recognize the need for controlled experiments and genuine research.

Bernard Grad of McGill University in Toronto has experimented with healing animals by touch. A healer, identified only as "Mr. X," proved to be of real help in healing experimentally wounded mice. When other persons touched the mice in controlled settings, their touches were found to be insignificant in the healing process. Grad separated the wounded mice into two groups. The cages for the two groups were identical. One group was treated medically and handled by persons with no claim to be healers. The other group was also treated medically, but not handled by anyone. Mr. X put his hands on some of the cages. The results? Handling by non-healers had no measurable effect on the healing process. But the mice in the cages which Mr. X touched healed more rapidly than the others.[3]

With the virtual elimination of preconceptions, expectations, and faith elements in healing in subjects such as these mice, the source of the healing powers of the touch of some persons seems to lie in the healer. But more experimentation is needed to test these indications.

Informal Touching

There is another dimension of touching in the process of becoming well-healthy-whole. It is related to the formal laying on of hands, but it is not the same. (Perhaps it is only a difference in degree.) This is the informal kind of touching that is the most basic of all human encounters—the skin-to-skin encounter. According to Sidney Simon, "...all of us have a basic skin hunger much like our physical appetite. We need touch as much as we need food. When we don't get it, something inside us withers."[4]

Much more generalized data comes from recent research on the beneficial effects of touching without reference to a recognized healer and with no association with the more formal ritualistic "laying on of hands." According to an article by Sherry Cohen, Emanuel Chusid, who is the Medical Director of the Westchester County Medical Center in New York, reports that a child who has Down's Syndrome will walk earlier if he or she gets a lot of hugging, touching, and stroking from his or her mother. She also reports that physicians at the Harvard Medical School treat cerebral palsy victims with a special touching technique that seems to be effective in reducing spasms and enabling more normal muscle action. Sick babies at the Rainbow Babies and Children's Hospital of Case Western Reserve University in Cleveland are helped when they are touched, held,

---

[3]See the *International Journal of Parapsychology*, Spring 1961, for a complete report of these experiments.

[4]T. and S. Emswiler, p. 18.

and stroked regularly by volunteers. Untouched babies develop *marasmus* (wasting away), according to several studies.[5]

The healing—"whole-ing"—aspect of this kind of touch is thought by some to be the ingredient of love expressed in the touching. Touching is love and care and concern made physical and physically felt. Sidney M. Jourard has pointed out that when a person reaches out and touches another, she or he is saying, "I want to share; I want to help." And when the other permits or welcomes the touch, allowing his or her "space" to be invaded, this other is replying, "I want to share; I want to be helped."[6] Or, as the Emswilers put it, "touch is the language of love."[7]

How do you feel about touching people? About being touched? Describe a time when someone reached out to you by touching.

How could touching be incorporated into a worship service in a comfortable, helpful way?

A persistent problem that arises when touching is encouraged is the "taboo" in our culture about touching. For some people, touching is regarded primarily as a sexual gesture. We usually apologize if we accidently touch someone—especially a stranger—as if to say, "I didn't mean anything by it." Even joining hands in a worship service setting makes some persons uncomfortable.

This discomfort stems partly from the issue of not having given permission to be touched. Touching threatens our privacy and may provoke a feeling of being manipulated. But deeper than that, the taboo against touching is probably

---

[5]Sherry Suib Cohen, "The Amazing Power of Touch," *Ladies Home Journal* (June 1982), p. 110. Many other accounts of the benefits of generalized touching are given in Ashley Montagu's book *Touching: The Human Significance of the Skin* (New York: Columbia University Press, 1971).

[6]Krieger, p. 82.

[7]T. and S. Emswiler, p. 19.

grounded in Victorian sexual attitudes. Basic in positive human relationships is a healthy appreciation of touching as a non-sexual expression of love and concern.

Laying on of Hands

A yet different insight into the value of touch goes back to a different use of the more formal "laying on of hands." This time it is not to heal but to transmit special spiritual power to another. In Acts, for instance, Simon "the Great" saw Peter and John giving baptized Samaritans the power of the Holy Spirit by the laying on of hands. "Now when Simon saw that the Spirit was given through the laying on of the apostles' hands," he tried (unsuccessfully) to buy this power for himself (Acts 8:9-24). This transfer of power was given to the Seven (Acts 6:6) and to Barnabas and Saul (Acts 13:3) for their respective jobs in the early church.

The practice of laying on of hands is very ancient and is found in many cultures. In primitive societies, it transmits "power" (*mana*). In the ancient Hebrew tradition, it anointed a king with the Spirit of Yahveh (1 Samuel 16:13-14). In Christian tradition it is called "ordination" or "commissioning."

Is there a connection between the *healing* power of laying on of hands and its *ordaining* power?

36

5 The Role of Prayer

Readings from Luke: 5:12-16; 6:12; 9:28-36; 11:1-13; 18:1-14; 19:45-46

How Jesus Used Prayer

Prayer is one of the special themes in Luke. Luke, more than the other Evangelists, emphasized Jesus' prayer practices.

Luke mentions a number of times that Jesus prayed. For instance, Jesus once healed a leper. This event drew crowds of people who came "to hear and to be healed" (5:15), but Jesus chose to withdraw into the wilderness and pray. One must suppose from this that prayer was an essential element in the ministry of Jesus. In another place, Jesus "went out into the hills to pray; and all night he continued in prayer to God" (6:12). The next time he did this, he took Peter, John, and James with him. As they watched him pray, he was transformed before them, and they experienced a vision of Moses and Elijah with him (9:28-36).

[handwritten marginal note: New Eng. says "soon time to time he withdrew to pray."]

In his teaching, Jesus stressed the importance of prayer. Two parables (found only in Luke) illustrate this. One is at the beginning of chapter 11, the other at the beginning of chapter 18.

The first one follows immediately after Luke's version of what we call "the Lord's Prayer" (the version in Matthew 6:9-13 is the more familiar):

> "Father, hallowed be thy name. Thy kingdom come. Give us each day our daily bread; and forgive us our sins, for we ourselves forgive every one who is indebted to us; and lead us not into temptation" (Luke 11:2-4).

Christians have used this as the model prayer ever since.

The brief appeal, "thy Kingdom come," and the petition, "Give us each day our daily bread," extend the concerns of the prayer beyond private and personal needs. In the sense that God's work is accomplished through human agents and in the faith that the Church is God's means of carrying out the divine mission, we are responsible for the establishment of the Kingdom and the supplying of that daily bread. Prayer, for Jesus, was never a substitute for action but rather the dynamic for action.

The parable following the Lord's Prayer (11:5-13) describes how an inconvenienced neighbor will eventually respond to a persistent call for help. The parallel parable (18:1-8) tells how an unjust judge will finally give justice just to be rid of the plaintiff. Both parables teach persistence, and both contrast God with the reluctant neighbor and with the unjust judge.

In the famous incident described in all four Gospels where Jesus drove out the money-changers from the Temple, Jesus quoted from Isaiah 56:7 that the Temple is a "house of prayer" (19:45-46).

We know that prayer was an important aspect of Jesus' life. But nowhere did Luke record that Jesus prayed in direct connection with a healing session.

In his second volume (our Acts), Luke recorded many acts of healing by the apostles, but in these accounts prayer is mentioned only once. In the story of Peter raising Tabitha from the dead (Acts 9:36-41), "Peter first sent everyone out of the room and then he knelt down and prayed...." (Acts 9:40). No further explanation is given.

What Is Prayer?

In subsequent history, however, prayers are both common and theologically sound. These include personal prayers for our own healing and intercessory prayers for the healing of others. Many of these have been formally structured into the liturgy. Many more are spontaneous cries for help.

The *power* of prayer is too well-attested to be doubted. The explanation of that power, however, is something else. There are many explanations, many "definitions," and many strange and wonderful ideas. A basic need of our time is to understand prayer better. Mary Baker Eddy, almost a century ago, spoke for today when she declared that "prayer may be a far more important field for research than neutron kinetics."[1] (Now we would say "nuclear physics.")

How important do you think prayer is in healing? Why?

What *is* prayer? How does it function in healing? *Why* should we pray? *How* should we pray?

Prayer is commonly understood as talking with God. It includes all kinds of talking—praise, thanksgiving, confession, petition, intercession, and dedication. Sometimes it invokes complaints and bitterness, and disappointments. In fact, it may include any kind of talk.

Prayer is also understood as meditation or contemplation. In this prayer, conscious words are not dominant, but feelings and introspective silence become prominent. Silence, quiet, relaxation, deep breathing, trying to be receptive to the meaning of God's presence—these constitute prayer for many persons. This prayer is more listening than talking, and it often complements the talking-type prayer in a real attempt to make prayer a two-way conversation.

For others, prayer is a life-style. It includes and involves action, actually living religious convictions. It may or may not include the more typical prayer definitions. For this action-oriented prayer, all of life is a prayer.

---

[1] "Message to the Mother Church for 1901," p. 1.

How We Pray

When prayer is related to health, and wholeness, and healing, it is quickly apparent that some prior concept of health processes determines (or at least influences) how prayer relates. For instance, if one shares the ideas of Oskar Estebany, Olga Worrall, or Kathryn Kuhlman—that they are simply agents for the power of God or Christ or the Holy Spirit—then prayers of petition and intercession are basic to the healing process. Healing is a work of grace. If one shares the ideas of Ambrose Worrall, John Sanford, or Joseph Murphy—that health matters follow strict laws—then the appropriate prayers are requests for a better grasp of the healing laws rather than a divine intervention.

> How do your own beliefs affect your prayers for healing? Write a prayer for healing based on your personal beliefs.

From some perspectives, prayer is less important to the healing process. If one believes the healer's power is somehow in himself or herself, then prayer in the conventional sense is not important. As one dips more deeply into the psychic aspects of health, prayer becomes less relevant also. Or prayers for physical health may be ruled out on "dispensational" grounds. Many Protestants believe that the healing miracles of Jesus and the early church were a special "dispensation" for the Apostolic Age and do not happen in our time. John Calvin, for instance, "emphasized strongly praying only within the bounds set by the Lord's Prayer, which makes no mention of healing as such."[2] Some modern evangelicals and liberals alike share this dispensational view.

Responses from a congregation of Christians will include several points of view on all these matters. Prayer in such a

---

[2]James N. Lapsley, *Salvation and Health*, p. 45. From *The Institutes of the Christian Religion*, Beveridge edition, Vol. II, p. 198.

corporate setting may have to be more diffused and general. For instance, all would agree that God favors health. As expressed by Steve Land, "It is always God's will to heal, but to heal the whole person and the whole creation according to God's own timetable."[3]   *disagree*

We can pray "in the firm conviction that our prayers make a difference," the Emswilers remind us. They continue:

> We are not saying that a gathered community's prayers can always bring exactly what we think we want, but such prayers can help to bring healing and new understanding, no matter what the outcome of the particular crisis, and we have seen these prayers transform the outcome.[4]

Group Prayer

George MacLeod also helps us to see the broader values of prayer, regardless of one's personal views on health. He notes that corporate prayer includes: "Prayers of confession for our own inadequacies, of active acceptance of our forgiveness.... Prayer is also always made for doctors, nurses, and all who, with us, are God's instruments of healing."[5] "Authentic prayer," the Emswilers remind us, "almost always impels us to action. Prayer is dangerous to someone who doesn't want to get involved."[6]

These prayer-values make it plain that, regardless of how one views the mystery of health, corporate praying is a valuable experience. Prayer taps into a powerful force. *(God)*

Experimental Prayer

Some persons believe that prayer-power can be understood through experiments. This belief is held by some

---

[3]Barbara McYahee Brown quoting Steve Land in *Ministry and Mission*, III, No. 3 (September 1978), pp. 4-5.

[4]T. and S. Emswiler, p. 53.

[5]*The Place of Healing in the Ministry of the Church* (Glasgow, Scotland: The Iona Community Publishing Department), p. 3.

[6]T. and S. Emswiler, p. 52.

scientists like Ambrose Worrall (physical science) or Anton Boisen (psychology and medicine). It is also promoted by some non-scientific healers such as Agnes Sanford. Boisen, for instance, believed that the role of religion in illness and health was poorly understood. Furthermore, it would never be understood properly until it had been "studied thoroughly by a sympathetic investigator."[7] This study would be an empirical study, based on controlled conditions.

Ambrose Worrall, who confessed to being "skeptical by nature"[8] favored "the scientific approach to all phenomena." He thought that "we should seek, by the scientific approach, to understand, to learn the laws governing spiritual healing."[9]

Agnes Sanford, a healer but not a scientist, proposes a "simple," "childlike" method, experimental in nature, and thus allies herself with the prayer experimenters: "One decides upon a definite subject for prayer, prays about it and then decides whether or not the prayer-project succeeds. If it does not succeed, one seeks a better adjustment with God and tries again."[10]

Since Agnes Sanford is also committed to laws governing health, her experimental prayers are necessarily petitionary or intercessory. If prayer fails, then there must have been a flaw (or flaws) in the process. We slowly learn the laws by experimentation, and as we conform more closely, results improve. She uses this analogy to clarify her viewpoint: if one turns on an electric lamp and it fails to shine, one does not say '"There is no electricity!"' One says instead, '"There is something wrong with this lamp."'[11]

---

[7]Hugh W. Sanborn, *Mental-Spiritual Health Models: An Analysis of the Models of Boisen, Hiltner and Clinebell* (Washington: University Press of America, 1979), p. 38.

[8]Ambrose Worrall, *The Gift of Healing* (New York: Harper and Row, 1965), p. 23.

[9]A. Worrall, p. 17.

[10]Agnes Sanford, *The Healing Light* (1947; rpt. St. Paul: Macalester Park Publishing Co., 1976), p. 6.

[11]A. Sanford, p. 8.

No need for guilt.

In the presence of a belief that good health is God's will for everyone and that the whole process is governed by strict laws, every failure carries the blame back to the suffering person. Guilt is added to pain.

This guilt opens the door to another way prayer functions in healing. If we confess our sins and receive forgiveness, we clear away some obstacles that prevent (or hinder) God's action in our lives. Our relationship with God is purified. We feel more deeply the presence of God and are able to function more effectively. Indirectly, this kind of prayer is related to good health—spiritual, mental, and physical. Steve Land defines it this way: "Our prayer for healing is a prayer to know this wounded, healing savior and to be in relationship with Him. To pray in the name is to pray in the presence is to pray in the will of Christ. And all prayer in the name shall be done."[12]

Not confess sin — but clearing one's conscience lendego the channel.

A very traditional viewpoint →

Discuss how physical illness might be related to spiritual illness, such as guilt.

Prayers for Healing

too fundamental for me

Francis MacNutt has a helpful practical analysis of prayer functioning to heal in his book *Healing*. In Part III he divides healing situations into four different kinds and gives directions for praying in each.

1. *Sickness of our Spirit.* This is caused by our own personal sin(s). The appropriate healing prayer is for forgiveness, with genuine contrition.

"substitute guilty & conditioned"

2. *Emotional sickness.* This is caused by the hurts we have felt because of the sins of others. Here the appropriate healing prayer is for inner healing (the "healing of memories," in Agnes Sanford's phrase). This is much more complex, and MacNutt recommends Mrs. Sanford's book,

substitute "mistakes or lack of sensitivity"

---
[12]Brown, p. 4.

The Healing Gifts of the Spirit (Lippincott, 1966).

3. *Physical sickness.* This is caused by disease or accident. Here the appropriate prayer is a petition for physical healing. [*handwritten: Substitute "claim health + positive thought"*]

4. *Sickness caused by demonic oppression.* The healing prayer is a prayer of deliverance, addressed to the oppressing demons rather than to God. It is more like a word of command (discussed more fully in this study in the chapter "The Role of the Word").[13]

The viewpoint that God (Christ, the Holy Spirit) is the real healer, either directly or through human agents, is presupposed behind the first three situations. The fourth is related to the psychic explanations of a healer's power to heal, discussed in this study in the sections on "The Role of the Healer" and "The Role of the Word."

[*handwritten left margin: No substitute - omit # 4 entirely.*]

[*handwritten right margin: No difference - all power comes from God.*]

In a later book, Francis MacNutt stresses healings that are not instantaneous but gradual. He has found more of this type than dramatic sudden healings. Because of this, he recommends practicing "soaking prayer."[14] A "soaking prayer" takes time and requires numerous repetitions (or treatments). It is not saying something all the time but continuing an initial prayer in song, tongues, or silence combined with the laying on of hands. Since hours may be involved, perhaps days as well, MacNutt sees "no reason why we can't pray for an hour and then take a ten minute coffee break before coming back to pray again."[15]

[*handwritten left margin: Curious!*]

Discuss the values you see in the practice of "soaking prayer."

---

[13]MacNutt, pp. 146-148.

[14]MacNutt, *The Power to Heal* (Notre Dame, Indiana: Ave Maria Press, 1977), pp. 39-55.

[15]MacNutt, *Power*, p. 42.

6 The Role of the Word

Readings from Luke: 4:31-41; 5:7-26; 6:6-11; 7:1-10; 8:26-39, 40-56; 9:1-6; 9:37-43; 10:1-20; 13:10-13; 18:35-43

Speaking the right words was another important factor in the healings Jesus accomplished. "In his ministry, Jesus took the power of words with utmost seriousness."[1] Usually the words used for healing were in connection with casting out an "unclean spirit." *needs defining*

"Word" in this section of our study is used in the ordinary sense of a word (or words) spoken to another. It is not "the Word" of the prologue to the Gospel of John. That conveys a very different meaning. There "the Word" is a pre-existent creative power that became incarnate in Jesus of Nazareth.

How Jesus Used the Word

In the first healing story in Luke, the introduction to the story reports that "his word was with authority" (4:32). The phrase "with authority" is the usual translation of a Greek phrase that literally means "out of himself" or "out of his own being." The words Jesus used were not based on some earlier authority, but spoken out of his own authority. He did not usually quote Moses, for example, or the prophets as the authority for his words but took the full responsibility upon himself.

Neither did Jesus speak the healing word in "the name of" someone else, not even "in the name of Yahveh." He was himself the source of his power. This self-source,

---

[1] T. and S. Emswiler, p. 21.

however, was not because of his intrinsic divine powers according to Luke-Acts. It was the presence of the Holy Spirit within him that gave him this power. In Luke's phrase, "the power of the Lord was with him to heal" (5:17). (See also Acts 2:22 and 10:38.)

In this first story, Jesus cured the man with the unclean spirit by speaking the word of command: "'Be silent, and come out of him'" (4:34). Those who were present "were all amazed and said to one another, 'What is this word? For with authority and power he commands the unclean spirits, and they come out'" (4:36).

The pattern is the same in the stories that follow. The central theme is the power of Jesus' word to command and to be obeyed. The dynamics are those of spiritual power; the superior controls the inferior.

Immediately following the first story of healing is another one which implies the same dynamic. Jesus was in the home of Peter in Capernaum, and Peter's wife's mother was ill with a fever. Jesus "rebuked the fever, and it left her" (4:39). The fever was understood as something that, when "rebuked," would leave her.

The story of the paralyzed man who was let down through the roof (5:18-26) shows the authority of Jesus' word(s) in a different setting. Jesus pronounced forgiveness, demonstrating his authority to forgive sins. This healed the man's lameness. Both the healed man and the people (displaying the characteristic Jewish understanding of miracles) responded by glorifying God, who had acted in and through Jesus. Jesus used only words to heal the man with the withered hand (6:6-11), without any mention of unclean spirits or forgiveness of sins.

A striking example of the authority of Jesus' words is shown in the healing of the centurion's slave. The centurion's faith was so strong that he told Jesus it wouldn't be necessary to go to him personally: he said just "'say the word, and let my slave be healed.'" Jesus commended him, saying "'not even in Israel have I found such faith.'"

The story of "the man from the city [Gerasa] who had demons" (8:27) is a full-fledged story of possession and

46

exorcism (although the official term "exorcist" as one who casts out demons is never applied to Jesus in the New Testament). When Jesus asked the possessing demon his name (8:30), the answer was "Legion," probably referring to the number of soldiers in a Roman Legion. Luke explains that "many demons had entered him." At Jesus' command, they left him and entered a nearby herd of pigs, which rushed into the sea and perished. *Did Jesus think so little of another of God's creatures?*

Jesus restored a dying child with the words, "Child, arise" (8:54). He cured a particularly violent case of possession by rebuking the unclean spirit (9:42). Jesus used both words and laying on of hands to heal the bent over woman (13:12-13). He healed the blind beggar at Jericho by the words "Receive your sight," but added "your faith has made you well" (18:42).

All these stories teach the authority of Jesus' words, especially his authority over unclean spirits (or demons) possessing individual persons. *bacteria, viruses, etc.*

How the Disciples Used the Word

gave her to predict the future

Jesus gave the twelve disciples "power and authority over all demons" (9:1). Later, he sent "seventy others" (10:1) out to prepare the way for his coming. They "returned with joy, saying 'Lord, even the demons are subject to us in your name'" (10:17). In Acts, the disciples continued to heal and to cast out demons, but now it was usually "in the name of Jesus." Paul, for instance, cast out the "spirit of divination" (Acts 16:16) that was possessing a slave girl with the words, "I charge you in the name of Jesus Christ to come out of her" (Acts 16:18).

From this beginning, the church throughout history has continued to recognize that "possession" by "a spirit," or "spirits," or "demons," or "devils" is a real phenomenon. Consequently, it has in its Roman Catholic and Orthodox forms, at least, developed rituals for exorcism and standards for becoming a qualified exorcist. In all of these, the principle has remained constant: it is the command of the exorcist, in words often formalized and addressed directly to the possessing spirit, that drives out the unwanted spirit. It is a struggle of spiritual power. The superior power of God-in-Christ (or the Holy Spirit, less commonly) forces the inferior spiritual power to obey.

Presupposed World-Views

How human existence fits into universe

Several possible "world-views" lie behind the whole notion of possession by a spirit and curing by exorcism. "World-view" is a somewhat clumsy expression to indicate the environment of human existence. It is a partial translation of the German word *Weltanschauung*.* English has no precise word for this. The French *milieu* comes close.

(1) The world-view behind the New Testament accounts is that of apocalyptic Judaism. "Apocalyptic"* comes from the Greek word *apocalypsis*, which means "revelation" (hence the alternate titles The Apocalypse of John or The Revelation to John). This world-view believed human existence was best understood in the context of a great cosmic war between God and Satan (see Revelation 12:6-12). With Satan defeated in Heaven (see Luke 10:18 also), the earth was the place of the final stages of the great cosmic war. Satan and his "angels" (or demons as fallen angels) were busily plaguing the human race (see I Peter 5:8). One or more of these demons, or unclean spirits, could possess an individual person and must be "cast out" for him or her to be restored to health. This world-view is well-documented in the New Testament.

(2) Another world-view lies behind the Gospel of John (which has no possession/exorcism healing stories), Colossians, and Ephesians. This is a Jewish-Gnostic world-view, not directly related to this present study.

(3) A still different world-view sometimes presupposed behind possession and exorcism comes from influences that see human existence in the context of Greek Orphic-Platonic thought. Possession and exorcisms were not related at all to the apocalyptic, demon-filled world of the great cosmic war but instead to the world of departed human

spirits who occasionally possessed a human (or an animal!) and needed to be "cast out." This world-view is assumed by a Canon in the Church of England, John D. Pearce-Higgins, who is "possibly one of the most knowledgeable and successful exorcists."[2] Such an understanding defines humans as essentially spirits (spiritual entities) imprisoned in a physical body that is not really part of our essential being (which is purely spiritual). This viewpoint is sometimes combined with a belief in reincarnation, as in the Ze Arigo phenomenon (see pages 61-62). Sometimes it also is combined with or based on Gnostic presuppositions (as in Christian Science).

Are Demons Real?

But is all this true? A large percentage (but not all) of the well-educated, mainstream Christians are skeptical and tend to regard demon-possession as superstition. The outward phenomenon is real and requires explanations. We need to re-examine, the skeptics say, the older traditional explanation of possession by another spiritual entity. This skeptical attitude does not necessarily reflect skepticism about Christianity in general or the Bible in particular. It is often the attitude of devout and sincere Christians who are loyal both to their church and to the Scriptures.

How can Christians be skeptical when some Scriptures are so clear about the reality of demon-possession? We do not need to surrender the authority of the Bible when we raise questions about the reality of demons; we do need to reexamine the Bible's authority and to understand it in a new way.[3] Many issues in our Christian past and present have not been settled by biblical statements. Some parts of the Bible sanction slavery, polygamy and the inferiority of women in passages that are very clear. Consideration of all four commonly recognized resources for truth—Scripture,

---

[2]Martin Ebon, *The Devil's Bride. Exorcism: Past and Present* (New York: Harper and Row, 1974), p. 200.

[3]See, for example, D. Nineham, *The Use and Abuse of the Bible* (London: Macmillan, 1976).

> Do you believe that "spirits" of some kind actually possess persons? Is exorcism dealing with the real world? What action would you take if a friend of yours came to you feeling like she (he) was possessed by a demon?

reason, tradition, and experience—sometimes leads us to a conclusion contrary to views recorded in parts of the Bible. Almost everyone now acknowledges this with regard to slavery and polygamy; most of us would also take this position on the inferiority of women. Others would express doubts about this biblical view of demon-possession.

The Bible itself has other world-views besides this late-Jewish apocalyptic one. It does not present just one viewpoint. Most of the Old Testament and some of the New presupposes human existence in a Satan-free world, ruled over by God alone. "The earth is the Lord's, and the fullness thereof" is the theme-song of the old Hebrew world-view (Psalm 24:1). Is the earth controlled by God or by Satan? Is illness God's punishment or discipline, or is it Satan's affliction?

How do these skeptics explain the outward phenomena? By psychological theories. As early as 1921 major studies paved the way for this current skepticism.[4] To explain modern psychological theories is beyond the scope of this present study. In general, they all call attention to the reality of personality disintegration, alternating personalities, multiple personalities, and other schizoid patterns. They all see the cure in reintegration of personality into wholeness, unity, and health.

The celebrated case of the exorcism of Anneliese Michel is a clear expression of this modern skepticism. She died in Germany in the summer of 1976 after priestly exorcisms conducted secretly at her parents' request with the official permission of the bishop of Wurzburg Dr. Josef Stangl.

---

[4]T. K. Oesterreich's classic *Possession and Exorcism Among Primitive Races, in Antiquity, in the Middle Ages, and in Modern Times* (New York: Causeway Books, 1974).

During months of efforts of exorcism, she was not given medical help.

Criminal negligence charges were filed against Anneliese's parents and the two priestly exorcists. Clinical psychiatrists were called in as experts. Their testimony largely determined the outcome. The parents and priests were convicted of "negligent homicide." Not merely convicted by the court, they were also "put down, ridiculed, and condemned by public opinion because of their belief in possession."[5]

On the other hand, there are some well-educated mainstream Christians who continue to understand the outward phenomena in the traditional ways. The French Catholic neurologist Jean Lhermitte for example, wrote that:

> ...what ever skeptics, unbelievers and the ill-informed may think, demonopathic manifestations are not extinct....Are we sure of the real existence of an "unclean spirit," an "evil spirit" who prowls around us seeking whom he may devour? There can be no Christian who does not give an affirmative answer to this question.[6] *Me!*

Lhermitte goes on to remind us of Baudelaire's famous words, "the devil's greatest cunning is to make us think he does not exist."[7]

Lhermitte's classic study distinguishes between true and false possession, however. In it he suggests that most so-called cases of possession are actually psychological disorders needing medical attention.

A similar stance is found in "The Possession Problem" by Richard P. Woods. He notes the "general sense of supernatural bewilderment"[8] that has resulted from the resurgence of interest in charismatic, spiritualist, and

---

[5]Felicitas D. Goodman, *The Exorcism of Anneliese Michel* (New York: Doubleday and Company, 1981), p. xiv.

[6]Jean Lhermitte, *True and False Possession*. Trans. (New York: Hawthorn Books, 1963), pp. 7-8.

[7]Lhermitte, p. 9.

[8]Richard P. Woods, "The Possession Problem" in *Begone, Satan!* (Huntington, Indiana: Our Sunday Visitor, Inc. 1974), p. 70.

exorcist phenomena, especially since the wide distribution of the book *The Exorcist* and its film sequel. "The problem with *The Exorcist*," he commments, "is not that it is bad, but that it is convincing, at least to the unwary."[9] He says that "*The Exorcist* case is particularly serious... because of the effect both the book and the film are having on a growing number of impressionable people."[10] Woods observes:

> The current heyday of diabolism is reaping much more than money; it is harvesting, or at least catalyzing, a whirlwind of spiritual and psychological disorders of frequently tragic consequences. A truly pastoral problem is in the making.... It is, simply, the problem of personal evil experienced as demonic possession, coupled with a desire, if not a demand, for exorcism.[11]

Fundamentalists, of course, form another group of moderns who affirm the reality of possession. Many of them, however, limit their recognition to cases of New Testament times.

Goodman sees the whole difficulty as one that is compounded by many other factors, especially the attitude of mainstream church leaders—one of "benign neglect"—and the prevailing skepticism regarding the reality of demonic forces and spirit possession. Finally, however, Goodman leaves open the possibility of real cases of demonic possession, noting: "While it is groundless to affirm that all such people [those who claim to be possessed] are possessed by unclean spirits, I would not rule out the possibility that some are actually so afflicted."[12] He does regard such cases, however, as very rare.

Another Kind of Healing Word

As a factor in spiritual healing, the word is not limited to commands addressed to possessing spirits. It also functions in less dramatic ways. Words of empathy, or understand-

---

[9]Woods, p. 67.
[10]Woods, pp. 67-68.
[11]Woods, p. 68.
[12]Woods, p. 75.

ing, or acceptance, or affirmation, or of love certainly function in a healing manner. They minister to real needs. They encourage and stimulate good health in all of its forms.

The speaker of these good words does not need special healing powers or ordination. The healing word may be spoken by anyone; the basic requirement is simply concern for the other. It is a willingness to be used by the grace of God for the redemption of those around us. It is the chief (or a chief) trait of the redemptive community. We cannot save ourselves; we can participate in the salvation of others.

In Protestantism we believe that this unordained healing word is a function of the priesthood of all believers. It is the principal ministry of lay persons, perhaps even the principal ministry of the church.

Also, as Protestants, we understand the healing (saving) word in a more formal sense. The Bible is the Written Word to be applied to the current needs by the Spoken Word, the sermon. The Written Word and the Spoken Word are equally the Word of God. We all understand the way the Word of God (written and spoken) brings us to "salvation"; we seldom permit the word "salvation" to have its full meaning, including wholeness and health in all its forms, both individual and societal. So the sermon is a healing as well as a saving word.

In what ways can you hear the Spoken Word (the sermon, for instance) as "healing" as well as "saving"?

The role of the word is thus an important factor in total health. It takes its place alongside all the other factors without becoming the essential one. The whole complex of factors is too intertwined for any one factor to be the most important one.

7 The Role of the Healer

Readings from Luke: 5:17-26; 6:19; 8:39; 8:43-48; 9:1—10:20; 11:20; 13:13; 17:11-19

Jesus as Healer

The Gospels make it very clear that Jesus had special powers to heal. In this chapter, we will examine the role that the healer himself or herself plays in the healing event. How much of the healing, or what part of the healing, is directly due to the special powers of the healer?

We can, first of all, acknowledge the reality of the healer's power. When Jesus was on his way to the house of Jairus to heal his daughter, a woman in the crowd touched the garment Jesus was wearing and experienced an immediate healing. In Luke's account, Jesus declares the healing event by asking who touched him and witnessing that he felt power go out from him (Luke 8:46). In Mark's Gospel, it is the Evangelist who describes the event as a power-flow from Jesus to the woman (Mark 5:30). That ancient explanation is still current as well as several others we will examine later in this chapter. The event, however, clarifies the role of the healer in the process of restoring an ill person to health and wholeness.

The Jewish Viewpoint

Jesus, as a Palestinian Jew of the Roman Empire, understood his healing powers as a typical Palestinian Jew of that time would have understood them. His explanation, as reflected in Matthew and Luke, was that God was acting through him. This was also expressed as the Spirit of God acting through him (the Holy Spirit = the Spirit of God). is there a difference??

The Jews did not attribute a healer's powers to the healer himself or herself. The healer was merely a chosen instrument of God. It was God doing the healing, not the healer. One way this Jewish understanding is revealed in the healing stories in Luke is by the expressions of gratitude to God that usually follow a healing. When the paralyzed man who was let down through the roof was healed, he "went home, glorifying God" (5:25). When the Gerasene demoniac was healed, Jesus instructed him, "Return to your home, and declare how much God has done for you" (8:39). On another occasion Jesus affirmed that his ability to cast out demons was "by the finger of God" (11:20). When Jesus healed the bent over woman, her response was that "immediately... she praised God" (13:13). When Jesus healed the ten lepers and only one—a Samaritan—returned to thank Jesus, Jesus' response was "'Where are the nine? Was no one found to return and give praise to God except this foreigner?'" (17:17-18).

What was implied in all of these episodes was made explicit in Luke 5:17: "the power of the Lord was with him to heal." It was made even more explicit in the second volume of Luke's work the Acts of the Apostles, when Peter described Jesus as "a man attested to you by God with mighty works and wonders and signs which God did through him..." (Acts 2:22). In another speech, Peter described Jesus as one who "went about doing good and healing all that were oppressed by the devil, for God was with him" (Acts 10:38).

In Acts, Luke went on to credit the healings performed through the apostles to the power of the Risen Lord. For instance, when Peter healed the paralytic Aeneas, he said to him, "Aeneas, Jesus Christ heals you; rise and make your bed" (Acts 9:32-35). The apostles repeated most of the healings that Jesus performed, including raising the dead, but always within the context of humans being the instruments of divine power.

Most modern Christian healers would share this interpretation (self-understanding) with Jesus and the apostles.

Oskar Estebany, for instance, explains his healing powers by saying that he feels he is "a channel for the Spirit of Jesus the Christ."[1] Olga Worrall instructs the healer to urge the patient to "relax and feel the presence of the God power flowing into every part of his [or her] being."[2] She and her husband Ambrose confess, "We know that no power exists in and of ourselves; we are merely the channel, the vehicle, for a power that is not ours to command."[3] Agnes Sanford agrees. She has described the healing of her baby's abscessed ears by a young minister as "the life of God" flowing through him for the healing of the child.[4]

In many other cultural settings, healers often understand their powers in a way that is similar in principle to that of the Jews (and Christians), but their religion requires a different name for the divine power that is doing the healing.

The Greek Viewpoint

Among the Greeks there was a different *kind* of explanation. Believing as they did in gods and goddesses and believing that these divinities took human form on occasion, the Greeks tended to understand a healer as a divine being in human form. A person with supernatural powers, then, was a supernatural being.

Luke gave us a story about Paul and Barnabas that illustrates the typical Greek viewpoint about miracles of healing. At Lystra the two apostles healed a man crippled from birth. When the people saw this, they exclaimed, "'The gods have come down to us in the likeness of men!' Barnabas they called Zeus and Paul, because he was the chief speaker, they called Hermes" (Acts 14:11). In Greek mythology Hermes was the messenger, or herald, of the gods and goddesses; he spoke for them. That's why Paul, the chief speaker, was thought to be Hermes. (Hermes may

[1]Krieger, p. 6.
[2]O. Worrall, n.p.
[3]A. Worrall, p. 9.
[4]A. Sanford, p. 3.

56

be more familiar to some readers by his Latin name Mercury.)

In the two Gospels (Mark and John) that reflect a more Gentile (Greek, in this sense) background, Jesus' healing powers were regarded as indicators of divinity. This is especially evident in the Gospel of John. For John, Jesus was one with God (John 10:30) and was himself the source of his healing powers. The healing miracles of Jesus were signs of who he really was: their function was to promote belief. The characteristic reaction to the healings of Jesus in John's Gospel was not to praise God, as it was in Luke, but to believe in Jesus as the one "from above."

The New Testament itself, therefore, gives us two explanations of the power of the healer, both conditioned by the prevailing cultural backgrounds of the times. In the Jewish explanation, it is God working through the healer. In the Greek it is the healer's own power. Today we are not limited to these ancient explanations, but we are obligated to consider the reality of the healer's powers in the cultural setting of the twentieth century.

Of course, the healer's own understanding of his or her healing powers is important data. It does not, however, have the same authority as the data about the healer's power to heal. The healer's explanation is often no more than the product of the healer's cultural and personal background.

The Power in a Healer

What is the source of power in a healer then? The healer's own explanation differs with the individual, the culture, and the time. Scientists have also explored this question. MacLeod quotes a scientific, verifiable healing event reported by L.E. Eeman, who described the cure of a patient who had been contorted by the effects of pain from acute sciatica. The only instrument of healing was a copper wire held in the scientist's right hand and the patient's left hand. After a few minutes in the relaxation circuit, he began to feel circulation and warmth in the affected parts. His muscles

57

began to relax spontaneously and progressively. Eeman described what happened next:

> Suddenly unbearable pain attacks him. He turns pale, sweats profusely and literally writhes in agony. Moved by his screams, I break the circuit and calm returns. I inform him that experience convinces me that, if he will but have the courage to face pain in the circuit until it stops of its own accord, he will be amply rewarded. He says, "All right, go on, I'll stand it." I close the circuit again and, almost at once, agony! A quarter of an hour, possibly more, and suddenly peace and relaxation. The patient rests and gradually recovers colour. His clothes are wet with perspiration. He rises, tests his limbs in various attitudes that have been impossible for weeks, finds no pain, and leaves the room almost straight. After half a dozen treatments in the circuit, this chronic sufferer from sciatica becomes a swimming enthusiast at the age of fifty.[5]

MacLeod concludes from this that 1) some force was present, 2) the healer was not deriving his power from any Christian belief, 3) "it was, nonetheless, divine healing," 4) it is similar to healings in a Christian setting, and 5) it does not always happen, either in Eeman's office or in a Christian healing service. This power therefore does not seem to be limited to people of faith:

> There seems to be a power in the world (it is sometimes apparent in the laying on of hands) which cannot be exclusively claimed for men [or women] of Faith. It is, none-the-less, extended to men [or women] of Faith at times. Some call it 'odic force.' ...Spiritual Healers, it seems, have this force to a marked degree....[6]

Ambrose Worrall had a similar opinion: "There is evidence that spiritual healing power is demonstrated through people of many religions, and through some who have no religious affiliations."[7] Nevertheless he also believed that the power to heal comes from "the Supreme spiritual power," whatever it is called and whether or not it is recognized.

---

[5]L.E. Eeman, *Co-operative Healing: The Curative Properties of Human Radiations,* as quoted in MacLeod, p. 7.

[6]MacLeod, p. 7.

[7]A. Worrall, p. 164.

Macleod points out that all Christians need to keep whatever contribution to healing they (we) have within the larger context of healing and not make exaggerated claims for it. "The Church is not the miraculous element in a natural world," MacLeod observes. "The Church is the interpreter of what is in any event a miraculous world."[8]

Do you think a person can be a healer and not be aware of her (or his) ability to heal?

Modern Research

While scientific inquiry in this area is still in its infancy, we have definitely broadened our knowledge about the role of the healer through experimentation. Scientists have discovered that Olga Worrall's skin temperature rises 13 to 15 degrees when she is in a state of healing. Other healers create a similar effect. For instance, one of the people who has experienced therepeutic touch reports feeling "deep heat... generated inside my body" when Dolores Krieger's hands were on her. Similarly, those touched by Oskar Estebany have often reported that they felt heat from his hands.

Scientists have also discovered that the hemoglobin level changes and the brain waves change in both the healer and the recipient during a healing session. This data was gathered during Krieger's carefully monitored experiments in 1978 at the Langley Porter Neuropsychiatric Institute at U.C.L.A.[9]

More data comes from Kirlian (*pronounced KEER-lee-an*) photography, a new kind of photography initially discovered in 1939 by the Russian electrician Semyon Davidovitch Kirlian. Ten years later, Kirlian, now joined by his wife, Valentina, had 14 patents and announced their new

---

[8]MacLeod, p. 8.
[9]Krieger, p. 9.

kind of photography to the scientific world.

In Kirlian photography the object to be photographed, together with photo paper, is placed between two electrodes. When the electricity is turned on briefly, an image is formed on the paper. No "camera" is used. The basic method is now refined and has developed into a special optical instrument that permits direct observation of the image that is produced (or exposed) by the electrodes.

What the Kirlians learned and have now documented photographically is that all living things—human, animal, plant—emit an active "energy pattern" that is not exactly identical with the physical reality of the living thing. This "energy pattern" may extend beyond the physical boundaries, may be expressed in many different colors, and may show a wide variety of effects.[10]

The Kirlians are convinced that living things have two "bodies"—the one we see (the physical body) and an "energy-body" that we don't ordinarily see. When a third of a leaf's "physical body" was cut off, for example, Kirlian photography showed an "energy-body" that was still whole.

When used to study healing by a non-medical healer, Kirlian photography of the healer's hands during a healing session shows a significant increase in the size and intensity of the "aura" surrounding the fingers. Both Olga Worrall's hands and Dolores Krieger's have exhibited this phenomenon.

Most of the studies either assume or theorize that there is some kind of "energy flow" from the healer to the patient. This explanation may have originated in ancient times from the feelings of the healer at the time of the healing. "Who touched me?" Jesus asked, "for I felt power go from me" (Luke 8:46). Ambrose Worrall witnessed that "a flow of healing force... comes often in... healing procedures from the solar plexus region of my body."[11] One of Krieger's

---

[10]The Kirlians learned to recognize a healthy organism or a sick one from their study of the color of its energy pattern. Prior to the appearance of any visible symptom, they could detect an oncoming illness.

[11]A. Worrall, p. 18.

patients reported, "'I can feel the energy flow she transmits to me.'"[12]

Dolores Krieger is one of many who have found an explanation in oriental cultures and their religions. Christians may, at first, reject such answers on principle, but, for instance, the Roman Catholic Church, in its Vatican II deliberations, did not condemn those of other religions who "look...for answers to those profound mysteries of the human condition."[13] Krieger studied the health practices of Yoga, Aruvedic medicine (Hindu), Tibetan medicine (Buddhist), and Chinese medicine. She learned that they teach that there is "a subsystem of energy which is called *prana* in Sanskrit...." She came to the belief that this best explains the "human energy transfer" that seems to take place in spiritual healing. *Prana* doesn't translate into Western vocabulary easily. It has to do with "the organizing factors that underlie what we call the life process." *Prana* is therefore what creates and sustains and heals life itself.[14]

Normally healthy persons have an excess of *prana*. Ill persons have a deficit. *Prana* can be transferred from a well person to a sick one. Hence the following model:

> Conceive of the healer as an individual whose health gives him access to an overabundance of *prana* and whose strong sense of commitment and intention to help ill people gives him or her a certain control over the projection of this vital energy. The act of healing, then, would entail the channeling of this energy flow by the healer for the well-being of the sick individual.[15]

This, of course, is a purely natural explanation. The healer's *prana* is the source of power.

A less "orthodox" explanation is the one illustrated by the famous healer of modern Brazil, Ze Arigo (Jose Pedro de Frietas), who was killed in an auto accident on January 11, 1971.[16] Although he hadn't gone beyond the third grade and had no specific medical training, he was a remarkable

---

[12]Krieger, p. 9.
[13]*Nostra Aetate*, Art. 2.
[14]Krieger, p. 13.
[15]Krieger, p. 13.

> Attributing healing power to one's God is clearly a religious option but would such attribution make the healing situation any different—or better—in the long run?

surgeon and healer with an international reputation. Ze Arigo was investigated by a team of medical doctors from the United States in 1968. The head of that team, Henry K. Puharich, came to regard Arigo as "the greatest healer in the world."[17] No other so-called "psychic surgeon" has been so carefully investigated and verified.

Arigo was a "Kardecist"—a follower of "Allen Kardec" (real name, Denizard Rivail). "Kardec" was a nineteenth century professor who believed in the reality of "spiritualism." For the Kardecists, this does not mean an organized religion, or denomination, nor does it encourage the more superstitious or ritualistic aspects of some spiritualists. They exemplify a sophisticated, intellectual type of spiritualism. Ze Arigo explained that his healing powers were due to a guiding spirit that actually did the healing. His guiding spirit was Adolpho Fritz, a German physician who had died in 1918. When Arigo was "possessed" by Fritz in a trance, he was the great healer. When he was not "possessed," he was a simple Brazilian peasant, loyal to his Catholic Church. He saw no contradiction in being Catholic and a Kardecist at the same time.

Many other healers have a similar understanding of their power to heal. One of the best known of these in the United States was the Baptist Sunday School teacher Edgar Cayce. Thomas Sugrue has written his story in *There Was a River*.

Why ? This explanation assumes the immortality of the soul and the actuality of reincarnation. It has many points in common with the understanding of what a human being is

---

[16]His story has been told in many places, most fully in *Arigo: Surgeon of the Rusty Knife*, by John G. Fuller (New York: Thomas Y. Crowell, 1974).
[17]Fuller, p. 210.

Raymond A. Moody, Jr.

in the thought of Elisabeth Kubler-Ross and Dale Moody as
they report experiences of those who reportedly die briefly
and return to life.

This "possession" viewpoint brings us back to the
Jewish-Christian understanding that the healer is an agent
of another power working through him or her. For Oskar
Estebany, Olga Worrall, Agnes Sanford, and Kathryn
Kuhlman, the real power at work through them is God or
Jesus Christ. For Ze Arigo it is Adolpho Fritz. The principle
is the same. The active powers are different. *Not necessarily —*

For George MacLeod and Dolores Krieger, the healer *the force*
possesses some special force. He prefers the terminology of *behind*
Baron von Reichenback and calls this force "odic power." *Fritz was*
She prefers the Hindu Sanskrit term *prana*. *God.*

> What difference does it make (if any) to regard the
> power at work in healing as Jesus Christ, or the Holy
> Spirit, or some other power? *Fritz?*

Becoming a Healer

How does a healer get to be a healer? The apostle Paul
believed it was a special gift of the Holy Spirit, or of God, or
of Christ (see I Corinthians 12:4-7), and not for everyone (I
Corinthians 12:27-30). A healer was a person with a special
gift. Francis MacNutt says that it is precisely a divine gift
and not a natural endowment that enables a healer. This gift
is "resident in God—the Father, Son, and Holy Spirit. It is
the Father, Jesus and the Spirit who heal. And they dwell
within each Christian."[18] He believes that "every Christian,
then, has the potential for healing," but "some people have
a special gift of healing."[19] *Why be exclusive?*

---

[18]MacNutt, *Power*, p. 90.
[19]MacNutt, *Power*, p. 91.

Dolores Krieger recognizes that healers are persons with a special ability, but she believes that this special ability can be taught to anyone. In this, she follows the lead of her teacher Dora Kunz. Dora Kunz, however, was born with a unique sensitivity to subtle energies surrounding living things, according to Dolores Krieger.

Church leadership in general, both the clergy and the laypersons, is not currently given any training in what Olga Worrall calls "the Art of Healing." Both seminaries and lay schools are concerned about spiritual and mental illnesses, and both offer courses in "Pastoral Care and Counseling" for the healing of non-physical illnesses. But the extensions of this concern to physical illnesses have been surrendered to the medical profession. Mrs. Worrall laments that our pastors are not taught the art of healing in seminaries. She freely acknowledges that there are charlatans who are "pseudo-healers," doing more harm than good. If local churches would include well-trained legitimate healers on their paid staff, she says "there would be no need for the pseudo-healers."[20]

Discuss how a healer on your local church staff would be (or is) accepted. Would credentials be important? If so, what kind?

If you had a healer on your local church staff, what impact would that have on your church counselling ministry? (or if you have one, what impact has it had?)

The uncertainties about the teachable elements in healing make implementation difficult. We may have to learn to live with these uncertainties. Many, however, would agree with George MacLeod that "concern [or love] is the secret of healing."[21]

[20]Hopkins, p. 3.
[21]MacLeod, p. 3.

8 The Role of Malady

Readings from Luke 1:8-25, 57-66; 4:23-26; 5:17-27; 6:17-19; 8:26-39; 9:1, 37-43; 10:17-20; 11:14-26; 15:11-32; 21:5-28; 22:14-23, 31-32; 23:1-49

"Malady" is a very general word, not commonly used. Originally Latin, it passed into Old English from French. In each case, it means "sick." The term includes all kinds of sickness—disease, malnutrition, feebleness, fragmentation (unwholesomeness), disorderedness. It applies both to persons and to society and includes conditions that arise from all sources, even accidental injuries. Incorporating mental, spiritual and physical sickness, it commonly includes all kinds of pain and suffering—physical, mental, and/or spiritual. It is an umbrella-word, covering a large variety of things that are subjects for healing. This chapter asks about the role(s) that malady plays in human life—and especially in Christian human life.

The Universality of Malady

Malady is the common experience of all persons; no one is exempt. Disease germs and viruses and bacteria are no respecter of persons. Headaches, backaches, and footaches are part of the larger network of aches that humankind knows first hand.

Malady is not limited to the physical aspects of life: it afflicts the mental, emotional and spiritual dimensions also. Mental anguish, hurt emotions, and the pain of remorse and guilt are also common for all of us as frail human beings. There is no way to become mature without making mistakes

65

that hurt us as well as others. It is profoundly true that "good judgment comes from experience, and experience comes from poor judgment." Pain and suffering are the price we all must pay for the progress we make in our earthly life. "Growing pains" may not apply to normal healthy physical growth, but no one can escape them in all the other aspects of life. Malady is a universal experience.

The Old Hebrew View of Malady

In most of the Bible, especially in the Hebrew scriptures (our Old Testament), all things have their source in God (Yahveh). Some of our malady is imposed on us by other humans in their use of the freedom granted by God, but this kind of malady is not a mystery. The maladies that have their origin beyond the human level—maladies such as storms, earthquakes, disease, famine, and birth defects— were all believed to come from God in the old Hebrew mentality. Yahveh alone was the source of all good and all evil, of both light and darkness (see Isaiah 45:7). Maladies from God even included those mediated by humans, such as wars and invasions. In this view, such divinely caused maladies were understood as punishment for disobedience or discipline to exercise our obedience.

Reflecting this viewpoint, Luke began his Gospel with an account of the priest Zechariah, who was struck dumb for a while as punishment for doubting the message of God given through the angel Gabriel (1:8-23, 57-66). The same understanding of malady is reflected in Luke 4:23-26, where Jesus reminded those in the synagogue at Nazareth of the famine God inflicted on the Israelites in the days of Elijah. It appears also in Luke 5:17-27 in the story of the paralyzed man whose friends lowered him through a hole in the roof. Jesus forgave his sins, the cause of his paralysis.

In this old Hebrew understanding, the cure for malady was repentance. If the trouble was God's punishment or discipline, then obedience and right living would end the malady.

✗ **Another Biblical View**

In the centuries just preceding the coming of Jesus, the people of Israel underwent some profound changes. Temple sacrifices were reestablished after the return from Babylonian exile (in the sixth century, B.C.E.) and, with one or two interruptions, continued until the Temple was destroyed by the Romans in 70 C.E. Even though the Temple was still functioning, however, the center of religious life was shifting away from the Temple to the synagogue.

Survivors of the nation of Judah, in the period of the exile and afterward, came to be known as "Jews." Away from Jerusalem, they formed worship and study groups called "synagogues." The leader (or teacher) was the "Rabbi." The new form of religion was "Judaism."

The intellectual and religious center of Judaism was not Jerusalem; it was Babylon. A thousand years later, it was still Babylon. The guiding principles of fully developed Judaism were formulated by Babylonian Rabbis and were collected together in their classical form in the Babylonian Talmud (ca. 500 C.E.).

In this Babylonian setting, there was a religious and intellectual influence on the Jews that gradually persuaded them to think differently about the source and function of evil and malady. In this newer understanding, probably adapted from Babylonian and Persian religion, the origins of malady were not ascribed to God (Yahveh). Human existence was more easily understood if Yahveh had an "enemy" who caused all the maladies. This cosmic "enemy" had even rallied an army of spiritual forces to dislodge Yahveh as Ruler. "The Enemy" wanted to take over the universe. It was this "enemy" that caused all of our troubles.

The Hebrew word for "enemy" is _satan_. Soon the noun "enemy" (*satan*) became a name (Satan). The post-exilic Jews began to think that malady came from Satan and his "angels" (spiritual forces in his rebellious army). It's somewhat confusing to have two kinds of angels, so Jews

67

increasingly began to call the bad angels (agents of Satan) "demons."

This "late Jewish" view (in contrast to the "old Hebrew" view) was well developed and popular in the Judaism of Jesus' time. Like the other, older view, it is also reflected in Luke. Most of chapter 21 is focused on the great cosmic battle between God and Satan. It describes briefly the troubles and tribulations that Satan is causing (and will cause) in these "last days" of the great cosmic war. Thus the famines, wars, earthquakes, pestilences, terrors, and persecutions (21:10-12) are not from God, but from Satan and his demons.

This view of malady lies behind all the stories in Luke about cures that are accomplished by casting out a demon or an unclean spirit. Luke reports, for example, that "those who were troubled with unclean spirits were cured" (6:18). The man in "the country of the Gerasenes" was possessed by "many demons"—a whole "Legion" of them (8:26-39). "The demons came out of the man and entered the swine..."(8:33). Another case of violent demon-possession is reported in 9:37-43.

Jesus gave his disciples "power and authority over all demons and to cure diseases" (9:1). Accordingly, Acts (the second part of Luke-Acts) records many instances of the disciples healing and casting out demons. In a report found only in Luke, Jesus appointed "seventy others" (10:1) to go ahead of him, two by two, and prepare the way for his visit. They "returned with joy, saying, 'Lord, even the demons are subject to us in your name'" (10:17). Jesus responded by saying "I saw Satan fall like lightning from heaven" (10:18), apparently referring to the belief that the cosmic war was over in heaven and that Satan's final fling was confined to earth.[1]

Among the disciples, Judas was "Satan-possessed" (22:3). Luke traced his betrayal to the Evil One. Satan tried to "get" Peter also, but Jesus intervened and saved him

---

[1]See Revelation 12:7-12 for a more detailed expression of this.

68

(22:31-32). All these passages make it clear that the source of malady was Satan, not God as in the "old Hebrew" view. The cure was not repentance; the cure was now exorcism.

Malady and Healing in Antiquity

In the Greek healing tradition, the centaur Cheiron, foster-parent of Asklepios, was wounded by one of Heracles' poisoned arrows. The wound was incurable but not mortal. Thus Cheiron became "the wounded healer." The wounded healer is more effective than the non-wounded one. His/her wound plays a positive role in healing others. The wound that will not heal is called the "Cheironian wound." It makes possible compassion (suffering with) and empathy.

A parallel to this tradition in Hebrew scriptures is found in the story of Jacob wrestling all night with his divine adversary. He emerged with a thigh that was put out of joint (Genesis 32:22-32). Then Jacob the Cheater became Israel. It was a changed person who healed the long standing alienation from Esau and became the father of the twelve tribes.

More to the point for Christians is the realization that our great Wounded Healer is Jesus. As Joseph Fichter reminds us, "...some Christians seem to have forgotten that the suffering of their savior was considered a necessary prelude to the joyful Resurrection."[2] Or, in the language of the Isaiah scroll that spoke so meaningfully to the early Christians, "he was wounded for our trangressions, he was bruised for our iniquities; upon him was the chastisement that made us whole, and with his stripes we are healed" (Isaiah 53:5).

Theologians have been occupied with the mystery of the atoning death of Jesus throughout Christian history. Their struggle to understand and rationalize our salvation experience continues. No "answer" is in sight. The mystery

[2]Fichter, p. 17.

may be permanent. It may be a perpetual reminder of our human limitations as we ponder the divine. But however we fail to see the whole, it is nevertheless true that Jesus is somehow our "Wounded Savior (Healer)."

A further example of the wounded healer, on the post-crucifixion discipleship level, can be seen in the Apostle Paul. He had some kind of "thorn... in the flesh." He regarded it, at first, as a handicap, "a messenger of Satan, to harass me," he wrote to the Corinthians (II Corinthians 12:7). He could not get rid of it. Like Cheiron's wound, it was not fatal, but it would not be cured: "Three times I besought the Lord about this, that it should leave me," he wrote (II Corinthians 12:8). But it didn't. Moreover, he came to realize that the thorn was not the handicap he thought it was but actually made his work more effective.

> If the "thorn" made Paul's work more effective, was it really from Satan?

What the "thorn" was is now unknown and probably beyond recovery. For our purposes, it isn't even necessary to know. It was probably what he referred to in Galatians 4:13 as "a bodily ailment," a condition that made him a "trial" to them. Beyond this, we can only speculate. Whatever it was, it served finally to advance the good news of God's salvation in Jesus Christ.

Shamanism

The whole pattern of salvation—health—wholeness by means of a savior who has suffered, died, and risen again is one that has several parallels in primitive religions. We understand these as "foreshadowings" of the Christ-event. Both primitive religions and the Christian experience come from a common universal need of humans, well discussed in the closing chapters of *Reflections on the Psalms* by C.S. Lewis.

In certain primitive religions, there are universal elements that are still practiced and yet are modern survivals of very ancient, pre-Christian ideas and rituals. Most appropriate for our study is the role of the "shaman"—a kind of a combination of doctor and priest. In less accurate but more popular terminology, a "shaman" (male or female) is a "witch-doctor," or a "medicine man," with special powers.

The classic study of shamanism is the one by Mircea Eliade called *Shamanism: Archaic Techniques of Ecstasy*. Eliade, a professor at the University of Chicago, studied shamans in many primitive cultures and concluded that one common way a person became a shaman was through a special sense of being "called." This "call" is usually introduced by a "hysteroid crisis," an ecstatic experience of some kind believed by the tribe to be the result of intervention by "the spirits." The emerging shaman is taken by the spirits into the spirit-world and taught the secrets that give the shaman his or her powers.[3]

Prominent in the early stages of preparation is a serious illness:

> That such maladies nearly always appear in relation to the vocation of medicine men is not at all surprising. Like the sick man, the religious man is projected onto a vital plane that shows him the fundamental data of human existence, that is, solitude, danger, hostility of the surrounding world.[4]

Not only is the emerging shaman inflicted with a serious illness, he or she also recovers: "… the primitive magician, the medicine man or the shaman is not only a sick man; he is, above all, a sick man who has been cured, who has succeeded in curing himself."[5]

In these cases, we can easily see that malady itself is not automatically an evil but has positive values as well. Sometimes it is necessary or essential to the health and salvation of the tribal members, who depend upon the "magic" of the shaman—a kind of "wounded savior"—a

---

[3]*Shamanism* (Princeton: Princeton University Press, 1970), p. 17.
[4]Eliade, p. 27.
[5]Eliade, p. 27.

precursor of the Wounded Savior himself. The Epistle to the Hebrews says this about Jesus: "although he was a Son, he learned obedience through what he suffered; and being made perfect he became the source of eternal salvation..." (5:8-9). John Sanford, commenting about people in general, says "there is reason to believe that in some cases an illness is a necessary part of a person's development."[6]

Modern Views of Malady

The biblical views we have already discussed are still alive today. The old Hebrew view that malady is divine discipline or punishment still functions in many Christian lives. The later Jewish view that malady is the work of Satan is also still popular among some.

Many Christians today, however, following a more modern approach, develop the ancient insight that suffering can have positive values. Robert Leslie says: "The Christian faith affirms the possibility of the creative use of suffering.... Psychiatrist Viktor Frankl, for example, described the positive role of suffering. Suffering is a part of life, he asserted; to remove suffering is to remove some meaning from life. Life takes shape through suffering."[7]

Of course, to follow this kind of understanding completely would make the whole quest for health, wholeness, and salvation a mistake. To be able to use malady creatively is a great insight. But that does not mean that all pain and suffering is good, to be welcomed and encouraged. It is obvious that most of our maladies are undesirable, at the very least. We live between the two extremes, usually seeking the cure but sometimes using the malady for our own well-being.

Often a serious illness provides an unparalleled opportunity for self-inventory and readjusting priorities. "Illness is a low-tide experience that reveals all the debris usually

---

[6]J. Sanford, p. 32.
[7]Leslie, p. 20.

hidden by high water."[8] After recovery, one's life may be in better perspective and the former illness may be seen as a blessing. Malady may be an invitation to wholeness, a positive step toward becoming a whole person.

Everybody knows, of course, that pain itself serves a valuable function. Charles L. Swan, now a retired missionary and college professor, tells of his experience:

It was from a wise old Mennonite doctor that I learned the meaning of *pain*, at least one of its many meanings. We were walking around the campus of his home for lepers—people suffering from Hansen's disease. It was in Central India in the days before antibiotics and the medical breakthrough on leprosy....

At a cottage for four men... a simple iron brazier was glowing in the middle of the room.... the doctor explained that Hansen's disease... causes the patient to become unable to feel pain in the diseased area.

A day or two before this patient had, unknowingly, placed his right leg against the red-hot brazier.... the hot iron burned the flesh deeply before he could be aware of the danger...

"See!" said the doctor. "Pain alerts us to danger... thank God for pain."

Further along the way I asked the doctor a question... "There are many dangerous and destructive things which are not straight-forward with their warnings. They do not cause pain immediately. In fact they are often 'silent killers.' Sometimes they masquerade as excitement and pleasure... what can we do about such dangers?"

The good doctor knew.... "Fortunately," he said, "human beings can feel the pain of others. It is a sad sort of leprosy that makes us lose our ability to feel the pain of others."[9]

Joseph H. Fichter has made a special study of the relation of pain to religion. He observed, "Human experience does not satisfactorily explain the prevalence of human misery. People often turn to religion as they struggle with these problems."[10] The religious question is not the one about the

[8]Leslie, p. 17.

[9]Charles L. Swan, "The Meaning of Pain," *Michigan Christian Advocate* (May 6, 1982), p. 2.

[10]Fichter, p. 20.

source of pain; it is one about the meaning of pain beyond its primary function of alerting one to danger. What is the meaning of chronic pain, and what is the religious response to it and to malady in general? Fichter reports three responses:

1. Pain is a mystery without explanation.
2. Pain is a blessing from God,
3. Pain is not from God and needs to be eliminated.

The first is a surrender of the quest for meaning, the second is the old Hebrew view, and the third the modern version of the later Jewish view that ascribes malady to Satan.

The ("New Age") Visions in Scripture

The Hebrew prophets were the severe social critics of their time. Seeing injustice all about them, they cried out in the name of Yahveh against the wickedness that violated the intentions of God. Part of their strategy was negative, proclaiming a coming doom as Yahveh's punishment. This actually happened. The nation was destroyed by the Assyrians and the Babylonians. The remnants of the once proud nation (the ten lost tribes of Israel) were deported all over the Assyrian Empire and lost to further history. The rest (the Judeans) were later exiled to Babylon.

The prophets then proclaimed a new emphasis—Yahveh's forgiveness and the coming restoration, a theme present in a minor way before this time. At times, this message was proclaimed so emphatically that the prophets were carried away with the idea and proclaimed a new golden age of universal peace. These utopian dreams reached their highest peak in the post-exilic oracles in the last part of the Isaiah scroll.

The sun shall be no more
  your light by day,
nor for brightness shall the moon
  give light to you by night;
but the LORD will be your everlasting light,

and your God will be your glory.
Your sun shall no more go down,
    nor your moon withdraw itself;
for the LORD will be your everlasting light,
    and your days of mourning shall be ended.
Your people shall be righteous
    they shall possess the land forever.... (Isaiah 60:19-21a)

And again,

I will rejoice in Jerusalem,
    and be glad in my people;
no more shall be heard in it the sound of weeping
    and the cry of distress.
No more shall there be in it
    an infant that lives but a few days,
or an old man who does not fill out his days
    for the child shall die a hundred years old.... (Isaiah 65:19-20)

The wolf and the lamb shall feed together
    The lion shall eat straw like the ox;
    and dust shall be the serpent's food.
They shall not hurt or destroy
    in all my holy mountain,

                                    says the LORD. (Isaiah 65:25)

These visions of a new age solved the problem of evil by eliminating it and were naturally congenial with the new ideas of the "Jews" (surviving Judeans) about God's victory over Satan in the Great Cosmic War. The "Revelation-literature" (apocalyptic literature) that forms the backdrop of the earliest period of Apostolic Christianity combined these ideas of the new age to come with the new age that would follow the end of the cosmic war. In the language familiar to us from the teachings of Jesus, the new age is the coming Kingdom of God.

This apocalyptic understanding presupposes that all malady is the work of "the Enemy" (Satan) and denies any positive values. In the last analysis, all malady is evil and slated for elimination. The Book of Revelation, the best biblical expression of these ideas, promises that God "will wipe away every tear from their eyes, and death shall be no more, neither shall there be mourning nor crying nor pain any more, for the former things have passed away" (21:4).

Even if we think about a coming new age that will eliminate all malady, we are presently living in the old age and need to keep our focus on our times. In our times, as we have seen, some malady is a positive value.

The Difficult Questions

The healing ministry, with its roots securely in the ministry of our Lord, cannot aim at the elimination of all malady in our age. Some of it is always needed as the price we pay for progress in maturation. But how much do we need? Who has too much and who has not enough?

No! [margin note]

When the healing ministry is actually under way, who gets healed and why? Is there any way to see which malady needs healing and which needs accepting?

Are there times when we need to induce malady (at least mental and spiritual malady) rather than always seek to "cure" it? It has been wisely said that the function of preaching is "to comfort the afflicted and to afflict the comfortable." Wellness and illness are so interwined, in our age at least, that they define each other. We all experience both. Is the church called on to keep them "balanced"?

Faith in the providence of God should not depend on our health. God can heal those who are sick and broken; then faith is easy. But when, despite our best efforts, we are asked to live with pain and malady, a deeper and harder faith becomes possible—the faith that accepts endurance, not healing, as a way of life and still praises God. Some of us are called to that kind of faith.

poor choice of words implies God can't or won't heal. [margin note]

76

9 Technique or Grace?

Is the healing process governed by laws of health? If so, then, as we master these laws, doesn't that give us the power to control the results? Health matters would then be cleared of their "supernatural" elements and God would be in the picture only as the designer and sustainer of these laws of health.

The Natural Laws of Health

A major part of good health does seem to be under such laws. We are increasingly conscious of the importance of good nutrition, vitamins, and proper exercise for the enjoyment of good physical and emotional health. Certain causes have certain effects. Our expanding knowledge about these causes and their effects supports the hypothesis that all health matters are governed by laws that we already partly understand.

Some of the "spiritual healers" of our time agree with this. Lewis Maclachlan, for instance, uses an example of a car which breaks down:

> The driver of a car who finds that the engine will not start does not hastily assume that the laws of nature have been interrupted, or attribute the failure of his engine to some mysterious exception to the universal order. If he is wise he takes his car to a garage where it can be overhauled by experts who will discover the defect and put it right. So when our prayers are apparently unanswered we should make a persistent search for the cause within ourselves...[1]

Christian Scientists also believe that healing in all forms is a scientific matter. Robert Peel explains that "Healing... is the gradual replacing of false concepts in the human mind with

---

[1]Lewis Maclachlan, *How To Pray for Healing* (London: James Clark and Co., 1955).

the pre-existent spiritual realities as they exist in the divine Mind, the only true consciousness...."[2]

Olga Worrall of the New Life Clinic advises those who want to begin a healing service in their church: "It is very important to teach the people about the laws governing healing. Spiritual healing is a science and certain rules must be observed, such as positive thinking, replacing fear with faith, the importance of love, changing the inner man, etc."[3] But Olga Worrall also cautions that "no one can promise a healing." All we can do is to "hope that if every condition is met with, a healing may take place." She stresses that healings happen in God's time, not in human time.[4]

Her late husband Ambrose Worrall, an engineer employed in his retirement as a consultant to a major aerospace corporation, favored "the scientific approach to all phenomena." He said: "...The quest here as elsewhere should be an open-minded search for truth about the eternal and unchanging laws of God. I believe that most so-called 'miracles' are... only the working out of these immutable universal laws on a higher level of consciousness and being than we know."[5] In an even stronger statement, he asserted, "Everything in Nature is according to law. We live according to the laws of health or the laws of disease. It is impossible to break any of Nature's laws.... Spiritual healing is a natural phenomenon. It occurs strictly in accordance with natural laws."[6]

Agnes Sanford begins her well-known book *The Healing Light* with a chapter called "God Works Through Us," where she says: "God does nothing except by law. But He has provided enough power within His laws to do anything that is in accordance with His will. His will includes unlimited miracles. It is for us to learn His will, and to seek the simplicity and the beauty of the laws that set free His

[2]Peel, p. 12.
[3]O. Worrall, n.p.
[4]O. Worrall, n.p.
[5]A. Worrall, p. 17.
[6]A. Worrall, p. 164.

power."[7] Elsewhere, Ms. Sanford writes: "A wise engineer studies the laws of flowing water and builds his water system in accordance with those laws. A wise scientist studies the laws of nature and adapts his experiments to those laws. And a wise seeker after God had better study the laws of God and adapt his prayers to those laws."[8]

Lawrence W. Althouse (a recruit into the healing ministry of Olga Worrall) expresses this viewpoint quite strongly: "All the practitioners of spiritual healing that I know believe that it is a law-abiding phenomenon."[9]

It is interesting to note that both the Worralls and Lawrence Althouse, with their strong affirmation of laws that govern healing, use the "gift" concept in their book titles. It is also interesting to see devoutly religious and dedicated spiritual healers, like those quoted above, committed to an assumption about the universe that has been given up by the scientific community since Einstein. The Newtonian physics of strict "cause-and-effect," backed by the philosophy of Immanuel Kant, is now violated regularly at the atomic level, according to modern physicists. In an age when physicists are dealing with mysteries beyond "cause-and-effect," some religious healers (as well as other Christians) are still clinging to the rationalism of the world before Einstein. As physics teacher Harry W. Ellis has reminded us: "...the assumption that the universe operates according to rational principles... is not only unproven, but unprovable."[10] *Why?*

Healing As the Gift of God

In contrast to those who regard health as strictly governed by universal laws, some healers, together with the mainstream of the church, have traditionally regarded healing as a divine gift. The healer Kathyrn Kuhlman

[7] A. Sanford, p. 5.

[8] A. Sanford, p. 9.

[9] *Rediscovering the Gift of Healing*, p. 36.

[10] *Presbyterian Survey* (April 1982), p. 9.

assumed this point of view. Francis MacNutt says it this way: "There is no one method of technique that always produces results: God wants us to depend on him—not upon a technique."[11]

"Grace" is our English word for the Greek word *charis*, meaning "well-wishing." It stands for an intentional attitude of goodwill. It is from the same root as the Greek word *charisma*, meaning a "gift." Theologically, grace means God's freely given goodwill, a gift given unconditionally.

Traditionally we speak of being "saved by grace." *Soteria* (salvation), like *shalom*, is a large word that encompasses wholeness, peace, and good health. It is easy to understand why orthodox Christianity has traditionally regarded good health as a work of grace. This recognizes that God, not us, is in final control.

Although the controls are finally with God, that does not mean that we can disregard the causes and effects that we have learned about health. The "laws of health" are valid, as far as they go. But over and above our efforts and our careful observance of such laws, there is a greater power that we cannot control but only acknowledge.

We can now understand better why healings sometimes happen and sometimes do not. The failure of a healing to take place may not be due to violations of the laws of health or not meeting all the conditions but to factors included under the umbrella called "the grace of God."

The questions which come up at this point are similar to those universal questions that always get raised by the concept of salvation by grace. Theologically, does God desire the salvation of all? If we are saved by grace, then God either desires the salvation of all and does, in fact, save all (universalism) or God "elects" some to salvation but not others (predestination). We avoid these questions if we abandon the concept of salvation by grace and believe instead that God sets up the conditions of salvation, leaving humans free to choose and to enjoy or suffer the consequences of our choices.

---

[11]MacNutt, *Healing*, p. 195.

In matters of physical health, some spiritual healers clearly opt for salvation by obedience to the health laws, using similar logic (and, in the following example, similar caricatures of the other viewpoint). Commenting about "those parents and teachers who... taught us that God often willed us to suffer," Agnes Sanford says:

> If we think of God as a heavenly stage manager, jerking us about like puppets upon strings, this is a natural and indeed inevitable conclusion. God can do whatever He likes. We have asked him to make us well. He has not done so. Well, then, He must like us to be sick. In which case, if we are logical, we will not only stop praying for health but also stop taking medicine, for who are we to go against God's will?[12]

This kind of thinking drives her back into the rationalist-legalist position: "...The lack of success in healing is not due to God's will for us but to our own failure." It is due to "...a natural and understandable lack in ourselves."[13]

This type of thinking adds guilt to the ailment already present and even runs the risk of compounding the ailment. In contrast, Steve Land reminds us:

> All healing this side of the grave is temporary and partial.... We're in the process of being healed along with everyone and everything else in the world, and every once in a while God gives us a foretaste, a flash of what the end of history will be like. We call it a healing, and inevitably somebody starts trying to figure out how it happened.... But healing is not a cause and effect phenomenon....[14]

implies God zaps

To understand spiritual healings as a work of grace rather than a result of some partially understood laws has several further implications. Most basic of all is the way our physical well-being is linked together with our well-being in spiritual and mental matters. All our "well-beings" are gifts of grace, essentially, even as we have traditionally acknowledged that our spiritual health is the result of God's grace.

I believe the opposite, I guess,

What if we are not well— what does that say about Grace?

[12]A. Sanford, p. 10.
[13]A. Sanford, pp. 11 and 8.
[14]Brown, p. 4.

What We Can Do

To assign health in general—all forms of health—to the grace of God is *not*, however, to remove the responsibility of doing what we need to do to promote and maintain good health. Our salvation by grace does not lead us away from good works but rather enables us to behave more righteously. The health we are given does not lead us away from health practices but rather enables us to do those very things that enhance the health we've been given.

The great heresy of every age in church history is the popular religious teaching that we determine our own spiritual health by the decisions and efforts we make. Reducing our spiritual life to such human dimensions blocks the greater power that is ours as a gift. It is the same with all other forms of health. To put ourselves in the driver's seat is to take over the role of God. That is the ultimate blasphemy. *Is that to say we don't take credit or blame for anything?*

The Two Graces

From the beginning of its history, the church has taught and practiced two graces with regard to illness. The earliest of these, stemming from the healings of Jesus, has been the grace that heals. George MacLeod, present leader of the famed Iona Community in Scotland, accurately notes that healing in the early church:

> was as normal as the Preaching of the Word.... This dual witness continued through the Medieval period.... This obedience dropped out from our Reformation witness.... Thus the healing of bodies, though, at first sight, it may seem an incursion into the present climate of our Church, is really normal. It is not an ecstatic Church that adopts it. Rather to neglect is to be subnormal.[15]

---

[15]MacLeod, p. 1.

It is obvious to every observer, however, that this healing grace has never been a panacea for all health problems. Jesus did not heal all the sick of his time, and the disciples did not end all sickness in theirs. In the constant experience of the church in history, it has continued to be "normal" that some are healed, more are not.

The Church therefore has taught and mediated another grace alongside the grace that heals. That second grace is the grace that sustains, or the grace that enables one to endure the illness or suffering or pain. In its preaching, the church has given much more emphasis to this grace of endurance than to the grace of healing, especially in mainline Protestantism. MacLeod said, in reference to healing:

> ...In so far as the Protestant witness has retained the practice, it has till recently become almost the prerogative of the sects: the Christian Scientist, the Spiritualists, the Pentecostalists, etc. In such hands, it is always in danger of becoming a heresy—that is, its over-emphasis upsets the balance of the full Gospel.[16]

What may be needed most, at this time in our Christian history, is a renewed recognition of the genuine tension that exists between the grace that heals and the grace that enables endurance. In that renewed recognition, there is some hope that the balance will again be restored. "There is a legitimate place for seeking physical, mental and spiritual healing as signs of God's activity, but there is also our belief that Christian life is a life of strength and courage in the midst of suffering...."[17]

An early example of this tension between the two graces occurs in the witness of the Apostle Paul. He prayed three times for the removal of his "thorn in the flesh," but God did not heal him. Instead he found strength to endure it, testifying that God's power was made perfect in his weakness (2 Corinthians 12:9).

---

[16]MacLeod, p. 2.
[17]Brown, p. 4.

Other Explanations for Healing

Medical doctors are aware that patients sometimes have recoveries from serious illnesses—even "terminal" ones like advanced cancer. In a religious setting, those with faith regard such recoveries as divine healing. But "miraculous" cures happen apart from religious settings and without faith in any supernatural activity. The uncertainty of healing, always present in spiritual healing circles, is also present in secular circles.

In secular settings, physicians call recoveries that medical science cannot account for "spontaneous remissions," or "spontaneous regressions." In 1959 surgeons T. C. Everson and W. H. Cole published a study of 112 of these cases, all they could establish since 1900.[18] In a more recent review of these unexplained cures, a team of doctors in Cleveland concluded: "We believe that no current theory offers an explanation."[19]

Sociologist David Hume gave another secular "answer" to healing uncertainties, substantially agreeing with secular medical opinion. He said:

> We hang in personal suspense between life and death, health and sickness, plenty and want, which are distributed amongst the human species by secret and unknown causes, whose operation is often unexpected, and always unaccountable."[20]

The philosophical theologian Paul Tillich identified one "ultimate concern question" as the problem of the maldistribution of pain and suffering. Within the bounds of human comprehension there is no answer. God is the "predominantly religious name" for the answer to ultimate questions.[21] Therefore, the mystery of the maldistribution of

---

[18] "Spontaneous Regression of Malignant Disease," *Journal of the American Medical Association*, vol. 169, p. 1758.

[19] George B. Rankin, M.D., Charles H. Brown, M.D., George Crile, Jr., M.D., "Spontaneous Regression of Hepatic Metastases from a Carcinoma of the Colon," *Annals of Surgery*, Vol 162, No. 1, pp. 156-169.

[20] Fichter, p. 19.

[21] Paul Tillich, *Christianity and the Encounter of the World Religions* (New York: Columbia, 1963), pp. 4-5.

pain and suffering is traditionally explained in Christianity by "the grace of God." In the same way, the mystery of healings and non-healings are questions of ultimate concern, answered in faith by "the grace of God."

doesn't make sense — Grace means well-wishing

> What can we do about the "maldistribution of suffering and pain" among individuals? among the world's peoples?

This, of course, is not just an appeal to ignorance. If life's ultimate questions are not answered on the basis of the fundamental insights of our religious faith, the answers are both superficial and false.

From the larger wisdom of the main forms of the church in history, we have learned not to ask the ultimate question about salvation in "either/or" terms—"grace or works"—but in "both/and" terms. The grace of God and obedience to the laws of health, taken together, bring us closer to the ultimate mystery of total health.

10 Wholeness and Health

Readings from Luke: 4:16-21; 5:12-16, 17-26, 29-32; 6:6-11, 43-46; 7:21, 36-50; 8:43-48; 10:38-42; 11:34-36; 13:10-13; 15:1-22; 18:35-43; 19:1-10

Good health depends upon seeing the wholeness of persons, the wholeness of society, and the wholeness of God. Partial approaches are actually the sources of much sickness.

The Wholeness of Individuals

"In this new era of holistic medicine," declares Elisabeth Kubler-Ross, "we are finally beginning to appreciate that the human being is not only a physical body but consists of an intellectual, emotional, physical, and spiritual quadrant."[1] We only become whole and healthy as these four quadrants are brought into harmony.

Luke shows Jesus relating to persons in this total manner again and again. This included real concern for their physical wholeness. He restored walking to the lame (5:17-26), sight to the blind (7:21; 18:35-43), straightness to the bent over woman (13:10-13), clean skin to the leper (5:12-16), a useful hand to the man with the withered hand (6:6-11), and health to the woman with the flow of blood (8:43-48).

Although these are all important, Jesus was not concerned solely about physical problems. His activity in casting out demons showed an equal concern for the minds of people. After encountering Jesus, the Gerasene demoniac was "clothed in his right mind" (8:35). Jesus also showed

---

[1] Elliott M. Goldwag, ed., "Epilogue," *Inner Balance: The Power of Holistic Healing* (Englewood Cliffs: Prentice-Hall, 1979), p. 319.

great concern for emotional health. He calmed the fearful and taught the value and power of faith.

And Jesus felt equally concerned about the spiritual part of a whole person. He knew that one basic cause of spiritual sickness was sin and its consequences. Jesus declared that the sins of the lame man were forgiven, and his lameness was healed. When Jesus was criticized for fraternizing with sinners, his response was "those who are well have no need of a physician, but those who are sick; I have not come to call the righteous, but sinners to repentance" (5:31-32). The story of Jesus and "the woman of the city, who was a sinner" (7:37), is even more graphic in portraying the healing ministry of Jesus to spiritual sickness caused by sin. The three parables in chapter 15 illustrate further the theme of spiritual health through repentance. Another story, found only in Luke, makes the same point. "Salvation" came to Zacchaeus when he turned from his cheating ways; his spirit was healed.

In Jesus, as the black spiritual puts it, "there is a balm in Gilead." There is hope and healing for "the sin-sick soul." In spite of their sins, "Jesus affirmed persons and thus opened to them the way of wholeness."[2] In all these healings Jesus demonstrated his acceptance of the sinner. Jesus took persons where he found them. By affirming them, he gave them the inner freedom to repent and move toward spiritual health. We can see an example of this in the famous Mary and Martha story (10:38-42). When Martha rebuked Mary for not helping in the meal preparation, Jesus gently affirmed Mary. Perhaps what Mary was doing met a deeper need in Jesus than what Martha was doing. One can only wish that the story included Jesus' affirmation of Martha as well.

Sometimes spiritual illness is not the product of sin but an emptiness—an awareness of a lack of something. Jesus maintained his own spiritual health by frequently communing with God. Luke stressed the prayer life of Jesus and

---

[2]Narka Ryan and Catherine Elkiss, *Luke: A Search for Wholeness: Leader's Guide* (St. Louis, MO: Christian Board of Publication, 1979), p. 19.

noted carefully the times when Jesus left the people for a period of prayer (5:15; 6:12, etc.).

Jesus' God-consciousness was so real and effective that he may never have experienced this personal "emptiness" we sometimes feel. On the other hand, if he was fully human, he did. Gerald Jampolsky and Patricia Taylor have observed:

> Many of us are finding that, even after obtaining all the things one thought one wanted in terms of job, home, family, and money, there still seems to be an emptiness inside. Mother Teresa from Calcutta, India, calls this phenomenon "spiritual deprivation," and more and more people seem to be becoming aware of this phenomenon.... There seems to be a growing recognition of a need to feel a sense of fulfillment within rather than to experience success from without.[3]

The "sense of fulfillment within" might be expressed better as "an inner sense of affirmation and acceptance by God," for this inner need is not one we can meet out of our own resources.

The psychiatrist Viktor Frankl saw clearly the interrelatedness of all the human components. He called the spiritual dimension of a total person the *noetic* dimension, alongside the *somatic* (bodily) and the *psychic* (the mental). He regarded the *noetic* as the area "most characteristic of the human being."[4] Health was not the absence of sickness but "a positive and dynamic striving for wholeness."[5]

Fragmentation is an excellent term to express the lack of coordination between the human "quadrants" or "dimensions." "Inner unity" is a fine expression for good health. William James, the psychological pioneer at Harvard, defined religious conversion as the change in a person from inner fragmentation to inner unity. Much of contemporary "therapy" is a striving for this inner unity and peace. It is therefore very interesting (and important) to recall the ancient meanings of this Greek word *therapy*: it means both

---

[3]Goldwag, p. 145.
[4]Leslie, p. 16.
[5]Leslie, p. 17.

medical treatment and divine worship.

Personal integration requires a *center* around which all else is integrated. The new term "centering" attempts to express this integration of all human aspects around a central core. Religion is the only center that satisfies all the complications of a total person. To be "centered" on God is to be unified, whole, healthy and holy. As expressed by Paul Tillich, "Religion is the state of being grasped by an ultimate concern, a concern which qualifies all other concerns as preliminary and which itself contains the answer to the questions of the meaning of our life."[6]

But how does a person become *whole*? John Sanford reminds us that the way "is impossible to summarize" because each person is individual. Nevertheless he does say that:

> To become whole we must be involved with life. This earthly existence appears to be a crucible in which the forging of the whole person is to take place. Our life must have a story to it if we are to become whole, and that means we must come up against something; otherwise a story can't take place.... If we stand on the sidelines of life, wholeness cannot emerge.[7]

The psychiatrist Carl Jung called this movement toward wholeness "individuation." He regarded "individuation" as the source of all true health, according to John Sanford.[8] It is a process that moves toward wholeness but never gets completed in this life.

How do we move toward wholeness? The classical answer from the wisdom of the church is that we don't do it; it is a work of grace—a gift of God. We can take some steps toward wholeness: we can face our problems honestly, confess our inability to handle them by ourselves, be open to real communication, and keep ourselves in the means of grace. And, we can be cautious about accepting any

---

[6]Tillich, p. 4.

[7]J. Sanford, p. 19.

[8]J. Sanford, p. 15.

"do-it-yourself" program for wholeness and health. We can do a lot, but, most of all, we need the grace of God.

The Wholeness of Society

We are all aware of the tragic "brokenness" in the social patterns of the world today, with wars, famines, and political tyrannies. Economic opportunities are uneven and unjust. Ethnic prejudices run rampant. Women face discrimination everywhere. Children, as well as the aged, are often abused and neglected. We need the healing presence of Jesus Christ in the problems of societal wholeness just as much as we need his powers in our personal struggles for wholeness.

Luke, more than any other Evangelist, was aware of this aspect of the Gospel. In the very beginning of the story, the angel told Zechariah about John the Baptist. He would turn the hearts of the disobedient to the wisdom of the just and "make ready for the Lord a people prepared" (1:17). In "the Magnificat" of Mary, the mother of Jesus, a vision of the intentions of God included scattering the proud, putting the mighty off their thrones, exalting the lower classes, feeding the hungry, and sending the rich away empty (1:51-53). Later, when Jesus read from Isaiah in the synagogue at Nazareth he selected the passage that defined his full mission as including "release for the captives" and the freeing of those who are oppressed (4:18).

In our time, it is not difficult to find captives that should be freed or oppressed peoples that need to be rescued. For centuries, oppression has been a way of life for minorities and for women. Today we can see more clearly that this is a priority for the Gospel. Society needs healing and wholeness fully as much as the individuals in society. The message of salvation is for persons (individual evangelism) and for societal structures (the "social gospel"); it is not for persons only, or for society only, but for both.

Jesus demonstrated a real concern for the hungry. The beatitude in Luke is not spiritualized as it is in Matthew. In Luke we have the blunt promise "Blessed are you that hunger now, for you shall be satisfied," and the parallel warning "Woe to you that are full now for you shall hunger" (6:25). The ministry of Jesus included the feeding of the multitudes (9:10-17). The problem of the world's hungry has grown to gigantic proportions. We Christians of the "first world" are now the ones that are full; people of the "second" and "third worlds," especially those of the "third world," are the hungry. Furthermore, as "first-world Christians," heavily invested in capitalistic enterprises, industry and multinational corporations, we have contributed to the problem. Now it is imperative that we Christians recognize our involvement in the problem and take positive action to contribute to the solution.

Part of the sickness of society is exposed in the injustices of our economic system. Jesus warned about the perils of wealth and had some kind words for the blessings of poverty. Choosing a beggar's life for himself, he was careful not to get involved in a mad possession of "things" that characterizes "first world" economy. The beatitude about this theme is also much more direct in Luke than in its spiritualized version in Matthew. "Blessed are you poor, for yours is the kingdom of God," paralleled by "Woe to you that are rich, for you have received your consolation" (6:24).

On one occasion, when Jesus was asked to settle a family quarrel over the inheritance of property, he refused to interfere. He gave this warning: "Take heed, and beware of all covetousness; for a man's life does not consist in the abundance of his possessions" (12:15). Then he told his famous parable, perhaps best preserved in the newly discovered Gospel of Thomas, about the man who built larger barns to store his goods, only to die without enjoying them. An even stronger word of Jesus is expressed in his blunt instruction (given in a context now lost), "Sell your possessions, and give alms; provide yourselves with purses that do not grow old, with a treasure in the heavens that does not fail.... For where your treasure is, there will your heart be also" (12:33-34).

Only in Luke is the difficult parable about the dishonest steward (16:1-8). It is followed by several explanations

91

(16:9-13) which may be from the early church. Among these is an awareness of the perils of riches, "unrighteous mammon," in contrast to "the true riches" (16:11). The conclusion at the end is typical of Jesus' attitude: "You cannot serve God and mammon" (16:13).

Only Luke has the well-known story of the "ruler" who was "very rich" which illustrates again the concern of Jesus (18:18-30). The disciples were instructed in the radicalness of Jesus' prohibition of earthly treasures and reassured that their sacrifices were nothing in comparison with the benefits ahead. In Luke only is the well-known story of the widow whose tiny contribution outweighed all the huge ones, because it was all she had (Luke 21:1-4).

Jesus gave us no sociological analysis of societal sickness. He probably would have explained it as "demonic." He did have a keen awareness of the problems of wealth and poverty and offered appropriate warnings about the selfishness of the rich and the ongoing needs of the poor.

Modern studies have demonstrated beyond any doubt what we knew anyway by partial observations:

> Poverty and poor health go together. ...The black segment of the population (in the U.S.) suffers most.... If the medical care is surrounded by inconveniences and reinforced by long waits and impersonal treatment.... For the poor, a visit for medical care is frustrating, humiliating, inconvenient, associated only with emergency and pain.[9]

Add to that the nutritional factors in poverty, and it is easy to see why individual sickness is augmented by societal sickness and why wholeness and health for both go hand in hand. MacLeod warns us that:

> ...It is near blasphemy to pray for [Margaret who has tuberculosis] individually when there is a known cause [damp rooms in slums of Glasgow] which we should be tackling at the same time. Just as it is near blasphemy merely to pray that Jean, Mary, and John should be released from a fear neurosis—due to the present atmosphere of war preparation—without concerning ourselves about the international issues that make for war.[10]

[9]Leslie, pp. 137-139.
[10]MacLeod, p. 10.

Another societal illness that the Gospel challenges and promises to heal is the tragic plight of women the world over. In a culture that was notoriously sexist, Jesus was bold enough to include women in his disciple-group. In Luke, a short section (8:1-3) informs us about some of the women in the group, and adds that "they provided for them out of their means." This brief statement makes it easier to understand the presence of the women at the crucifixion and the crucial role they played at the empty tomb.

Luke paid more attention to women than did the other Gospel. What little we do have in the Gospels about the role of women has probably survived from a larger body of information.

On a more subtle level, Luke arranged the materials of his story in a special way which revealed his concern for women. Events and parables about men were sometimes "paired" with another event or parable about women. Elizabeth and Zechariah were "paired" with Mary and Joseph. Simeon is "paired" with Anna (2:25-38). Jesus healed a demon-possessed man (4:31-37) and then healed Peter's mother-in-law (4:38-39). Jesus healed a centurion's slave (7:1-10) and then raised up the widow's son (7:11-17). Insights about John the Baptizer (7:24-35) were followed immediately by insights from the attentions of the sinful woman (7:36-50). The Gerasene demoniac (8:26-39) was "paired" with the healing of Jairus' daughter and the woman with the flow of blood (8:40-56). The Good Samaritan parable (10:25-37) was "paired" with the Mary-Martha incident (10:38-42). Sandwiched between the parable of the lost sheep and the Prodigal Son was the woman with the lost coin. While the pairing cannot be seen as a rigid structure, it does reveal an unusual concern on the part of Luke to "give equal time" to women in the story.

So, in addition to Jesus, Luke may also have contributed to the healing of society's sexual brokenness through the perspective he chose to use in his Gospel. Although both contributed to the solution to society's injustice to women, they did not provide our final answer. What they did do was to point out the direction we need to take.

Our newly advanced sensitivity to the rights of women has a long way to go before we reach the desired end, but the direction is clear from the example of our Lord and the emphasis of Luke: we must follow it. Again, wholeness of women in society requires the wholeness of society itself. The healing of the person is impossible without the healing of the system.

What We Can Do

In United Methodist circles, all Christians are ministers, a few of whom are called to be pastors. Every Christian is called to ministry. What is ministry? It is the mediation of salvation. What is salvation? It is *shalom*, peace, wholeness, health. It is more than a spiritual condition. It is a total condition, involving all of us—body, mind, emotions, and spirit.

In our common call to minister, Jesus is our model. From the wholeness of his ministry, we get our vision of a holistic ministry. This vision calls us into healing the isolation and brokenness of individuals. Whatever the brokenness is, whether physical, mental, emotional, or spiritual, it is the object of our ministry. We participate in a redemptive community, and the grace of God works through us for others and through others for us. We can participate in that redemptive community.

But ministry to individual brokenness is not the whole mission. We are called to minister to the brokenness of society also. Individual wholeness and societal wholeness are intimately related. Our ministry calls us to oppose the social systems that permit, or even cause, hunger, poverty, racism, sexism, agism, and all the other signs of societal brokenness. This means active involvement in "worldly affairs" such as politics and economics and power struggles. Real involvement may mean the path of the cross.

Salvation—wholeness and total health—may be, in the last analysis, a free gift of God, a work of grace. It must be recognized, however, that salvation is not "cheap grace" but a call to costly discipleship.

Bibliography

Books marked with a double asterisk are highly recommended by the author.

Althouse, Lawrence W. *Rediscovering the Gift of Healing*. Nashville: Abingdon Press, 1977.

Barrett, C. K. *Luke the Historian in Recent Study*. Philadelphia: Fortress Press, 1970. (Facet Books: Biblical Series No. 24, revision of 1961 lecture).**

Campbell, Joseph. *Myths to Live By*. New York: Viking, 1972.

A Century of Christian Science Healing. Boston: The Christian Science Publishing Society, 1966.

Christ, Carol P. and Judith Plaskow. Eds. *Womanspirit Rising*. San Francisco: Harper and Row, 1979.

Clinebell, Howard John. Ed. *Community Mental Health*. Nashville: Abingdon Press, 1970.

Conzelmann, Hans. *An Outline of the Theology of the New Testament*. 2nd edition. Trans. John Bowden. New York: Harper and Row, 1969.**

Conzelmann, Hans. *The Theology of St. Luke*. Trans. Geoffrey Buswell. London: Faber and Faber, 1960.

Cousins, Norman. *Anatomy of an Illness*. 1979; rpt. New York: Bantam, 1981.

Creed, John Martin. *The Gospel According to Luke*. London: Macmillan and Co., 1930.**

Danker, Frederick W. *Jesus and the New Age According to St. Luke: A Commentary on the Third Gospel*. St. Louis: Clayton, 1972.

Danker, Frederick W. *Luke*. Philadelphia: Fortress Press, 1976.

Dibelius, Martin. *Studies in the Acts of the Apostles*. Ed. H. Greeven. Trans. Mary Ling. New York: Scribner's, 1956.**

Easton, Burton Scott. *Early Christianity: The Purpose of Acts and other Papers*. London: S.P.C.K., 1955.**

Ebon, Martin. *The Devil's Bride. Exorcism: Past and Present*. New York: Harper and Row, 1974.

Ellis, Earle E. *Eschatology in Luke*. Philadelphia: Fortress Press, 1972.

Emswiler, Thomas Neufer and Sharon Neufer Emswiler. *Wholeness in Worship*. San Francisco: Harper and Row, 1980.**

Fichter, Joseph H. *Religion and Pain*. New York: Crossroad, 1981.

Franklin, Eric. *Christ the Lord: A Study in the Purpose and Theology of Luke-Acts*. Philadelphia: Westminster, 1975.

Frazier, Claude A. Ed. *Healing and Religious Faith*. Philadelphia: United Church Press, 1974.

Fuller, John G. *Arigo: Surgeon of the Rusty Knife*. New York: Thomas Y. Crowell Co., 1974.**

Giles, Mary E. Ed. *The Feminist Mystic*. New York: Crossroad, 1982.

Goldwag, Elliott M. Ed. *Inner Balance: The Power of Holistic Healing*. Englewood Cliffs: Prentice-Hall, 1979.**

Goodman, Felicitas D. *The Exorcism of Anneliese Michel*. New York: Doubleday and Co., 1981.**

Haenchen, Ernst. *The Acts of the Apostles*. Trans. from the 14th edition of the German under the supervision of Hugh Anderson. Rev. by R. Mc. L. Wilson. Philadelphia: Westminster, 1971.**

Jackson, F.J. Foakes and Kirsopp Lake. Eds. *The Beginnings of Christianity*, Part I, The Acts of the Apostles (5 vols). London: MacMillan and Co., 1933.**

Jeremias, Joachim. *The Parables of Jesus*. Revised Edition. Trans. S.H. Hooke. New York: Charles Scribner's Sons, 1963.**

Keck, Leander E. and J. Louis Martyn. Eds. *Studies in Luke-Acts*. Nashville: Abingdon Press, 1966.**

Kelsey, Morton T. *Healing and Christianity in Ancient Thought and Modern Times*. New York: Harper and Row, 1973.**

Krieger, Dolores. *The Therapeutic Touch*. Englewood Cliffs, New Jersey: Prentice-Hall, 1980.**

Kuhlman, Kathryn. *God Can Do It Again*. Englewood Cliffs, New Jersey: Prentice-Hall, 1969.

Kuhlman, Kathryn. *Nothing is Impossible with God*. Englewood Cliffs, New Jersey: Prentice-Hall, Inc., 1974.

Leslie, Robert C. *Health, Healing and Holiness*. Nashville: Graded Press, 1971.**

Lhermitte, Jean. *True and False Possession*. Trans. New York: Hawthorn Books, 1963.**

Linn, Matthew, S.J., and Dennis Linn, S.J. *The Healing of Memories*. New York: Paulist Press, 1974.

MacLeod, George. *The Place of Healing in the Ministry of the Church*. Glasgow, Scotland: The Iona Community Publishing Department, n.d.**

MacNutt, Francis. *Healing*. Indiana: Ave Maria Press, 1974.**

MacNutt, Francis. *The Power to Heal*. Notre Dame, Indiana: Ave Maria Press, 1977.**

Marty, Martin E. and Kenneth L. Vaux. Eds. *Health/Medicine and the Faith Traditions: An Inquiry into Religion and Medicine*. Philadelphia: Fortress Press, 1982.**

Montagu, Ashley. *Touching: The Human Significance of the Skin*. New York: Columbia University Press, 1971.

Nineham, Dennis. *The Use and Abuse of the Bible*. London: Macmillan, 1976.**

Nouwen, Henri, J.M. *The Wounded Healer*. 1972; rpt. Garden City, New York: Image Books, 1979.

Ostrander, Sheila and Lynn Schroeder. *Psychic Discoveries Behind the Iron Curtain*. 1970; rpt. Englewood Cliffs, New Jersey: Bantam, 1971.**

Phipps, William E. *Recovering Biblical Sensuousness*. Philadelphia: Westminster, 1975.

Rose, Louis. *Faith Healing*. 1968; rpt. New York: Penguin Books, 1971.

Sanborn, Hugh W. *Mental-Spiritual Health Models: An Analysis of the Models of Boisen, Hiltner and Clinebell*. Washington: University Press of America, 1979.**

Sanford, Agnes. *The Healing Light*. Rev. Ed. St. Paul, MN: Macalester Park, 1972.

Sanford, John A. *Healing and Wholeness*. New York: Paulist Press, 1977.**

Simson, Eve. *The Faith Healer*. New York: Pyramid Publications (Harcourt Brace Jovanovich, Inc.), 1977.

Swift, Edgar J. *Jungle of the Mind*. Facsimile edition (Essay Index Reprint. Series Reproduction of 1931 ed.).

Tillich, Paul. *Christianity and Encounter of the World Religions*. New York: Columbia, 1963.

Tournier, Paul. *The Healing of Persons*. Trans. Edwin Hudson. New York: Harper and Row, 1965.**

Woods, Richard P. "The Possession Problem," in *Begone, Satan!*. Huntington: IN: Our Sunday Visitor, Inc., 1974.**

Worrall, Ambrose, with Olga N. Worrall. *The Gift of Healing*. New York: Harper and Row, 1965.

Teacher's Guide

by Nancy A. Carter

Planning the Study.. 99

Study Session I..103

Study Session II...105

Study Session III...109

Study Session IV...112

Study Session V..115

Study Session VI...118

Study Session VII.. 121

Study Session VIII...123

Study Session IX...126

Study Session X..129

Shortening the Number of Study Sessions......................133

The Author

Nancy A. Carter is editor of program resources for the Education and Cultivation Division of the General Board of Global Ministries of The United Methodist Church. She edited the text *The Great Physician* and wrote the script for the slide set on Luke. She has a Ph.D. in literary studies (literature and theology) from American University in Washington, D.C. and has done additional graduate work at Wesley Theological Seminary and Union Theological Seminary.

PLANNING THE STUDY

Resources

This *Teacher's Guide* offers groups an opportunity to use a variety of approaches to this year's theme. The basic text for the theme Luke on Wholeness, Healing, Holiness, and Wholeness of Life is *The Great Physician* (#4251, $1.50)* by Lindsey P. Pherigo. Two other basic resources are the Bible, of course, and the Luke Slide Set (#4255, $7.50).* This year, the Women's Division is making available for this study a large print edition of Luke *Good News By a Man Named Luke* (#4236, $1.25).* You may wish to order copies of these. Persons who have trouble reading smaller print will appreciate them. Others may wish to use them as study books and write in them. (They might not want to write in their personal Bibles.)

Use of the Text and the Guide

There are a number of approaches that you, as a teacher, may choose to take. (If possible, make your decisions in consultation with the members of the study group.) One approach would be to use only the text and the Bible, asking the questions which have been placed in the chapters by the author. You could either assign the chapters for reading before class or read them in class and discuss the questions. The latter approach tends to bore a group, but sometimes circumstances make it necessary. Another approach could be to include more Bible study than the text does. If your class would like to explore further certain biblical passages related to these chapters, then you will wish to consult the additional material in this guide. Yet another approach would be to involve the class in certain group exercises, such as role play, guided meditation, and drawing, as a means of conveying the theme of wholeness. Usually, discussion questions are "head" exercises; whereas group exercises such as those just mentioned are "heart" exercises.

---

*In this guide all resources marked with an asterisk are available from the Service Center, 7820 Reading Road, Cincinnati, Ohio 45237. Consult the *Catalog* for prices.

The group needs to involve both its head and its heart in this study to truly understand its meaning. Probably, you will create some combination of all of the above approaches because it is usually good to use many different approaches when teaching a class.

Preparation by the Leader

Before leading the study, read both *The Great Physician** and the Gospel According to Luke. You might keep a journal of notes and reflections about your reading of these to help guide your preparation and teaching of the course. Continue your journal until the end of the class. After the class is finished, re-read the journal and write your reflections on your notes and your experiences. You will probably discover that the old saying that a teacher learns more than the students is true. For more information about keeping a journal, see *Live the Questions Now: The Interior Life* (#3609, $1.75).*

In addition to the text and Luke, read books about wholeness, healing, and Luke. An easily read overview of Luke written for laypersons is *Luke's Story of Jesus* (Philadelphia: Fortress Press, 1981) by O. C. Edwards, Jr. For information on the theme of healing, Francis MacNutt's *Healing* (1974; rpt. New York: Bantam Books, 1980) and *The Power to Heal* (Notre Dame, Indiana: Ave Maria Press, 1978) are valuable resources. They are written from a Roman Catholic perspective, so some material will be less valuable to a United Methodist. Another good book, which was on United Methodist Women's Reading List a number of years ago and may therefore be in the church's library, is Morton Kelsey's *Healing and Christianity* (New York: Harper and Row, 1973). It gives valuable historical information about healing and wholeness. John A. Sanford's *Healing and Wholeness* (New York: Paulist Press, 1977) is also good. For a discussion of societal wholeness, read *Jesus, Politics and Society: A Study of Luke's Gospel* (Maryknoll, New York: Orbis Books, 1978) by Richard J. Cassidy. The bibliography in the basic text lists many other possibilities.

Of course, reading of these books need not be limited to

the leader. You may wish people to read portions of these and report on them to the group.

After you have done your basic preparation, explore with the members or potential members of the class their needs and hopes for a study such as this one. Develop your plans with them. As you proceed with the study, other needs will emerge. Be flexible enough to change your plans to include these new things.

Supplies and Resources for Use in the Class

1. Each member should have a copy of *The Great Physician** and a Bible or *Good News By a Man Named Luke.**

2. For each session, keep extra Bibles on hand in case some members forget to bring one. Include a variety of translations, especially those suggested by Lindsey Pherigo in the "Author's Foreword." A few commentaries such as *The Interpreter's Bible,* Volume 8, *The Interpreter's One-Volume Commentary on the Bible,* William Barclay's *The Gospel of Luke,* revised edition (Philadelphia: Westminster Press, 1975), G. B. Caird's *Saint Luke* (New York: Penguin Books, 1963), and Charles R. Erdman's *The Gospel of Luke* (Philadelphia: Westminster Press, 1966) would be helpful to have on hand.

3. Other valuable reference works are *The Interpreter's Dictionary of the Bible* (4 volumes, plus the supplement) and a good concordance.

4. If you approach your study by comparing and contrasting some of the Gospel parallels to the healing stories in Luke, you may wish to use *Gospel Parallels,* revised (Nashville: Thomas Nelson, 1967), edited by Burton H. Throckmorton, Jr.

5. Have in the class worship resources such as the ones listed in the sessions which follow. *Sisters and Brothers Sing!,* *Wholeness in Worship, Images: Women in Transition, The Healing Fountain,* and *Live the Questions Now* are all available from the Service Center. *The Book of Hymns,* and *Songs of Zion* are available from Cokesbury. *Celebremos* I is available from Discipleship Resources.

6. If the class will be doing work on newsprint, make this resource available along with materials such as magic markers, crayons, masking tape, and scissors.

Setting for the Class

An attractive room aids a class's study experience. An ideal situation would be to meet in a room with moveable chairs, some tables, a blackboard, bulletin boards, an easel, and good lighting. It should be a place where you can hang displays, but if the room is shared with other groups, this may not be possible. Sometimes you may not have much choice about the type of room in which you meet; then you must make the best of it. This writer has taught in places such as a lounge with couches (no moveable chairs, tables, blackboards, etc.), a library, a cafeteria (no possibility of displays), and a music room which had desks set on tiers. Still she was able to divide the classes into small groups, improvise displays on easels or draped over grand pianos (not taped down, of course), and so on. Make the best use of your situation.

The Study Sessions

The following material includes suggestions for study. Feel free to use and adapt what you need. This guide suggests ten sessions of study. Increase or decrease the number and length of them according to your needs. (See the chapter "Shortening the Number of Study Sessions" for suggestions.) Please note that most sessions include more suggestions than you could possibly use in the space of one or two hours. Don't try to do them all in that time! Select those which seem most appropriate to your group.

Each session begins with suggestions for reading, reports, displays, hymns, and prayers, and keeping a journal. Use these as they appear or as inspiration for your own approach. The exercises for keeping a journal are intended for individual work at home, but you may wish to set a separate time for interested people to come and write in their journals as a group. They can either share or keep private their entries according to their individual desires.

STUDY SESSION I

Assignments

Reading: Read the foreword in the text.

Art: You may wish to display some quotes on construction paper around the meeting room. These could include quotes from the text, such as "Health exists when body, mind, and spirit work in harmony" and "Those who want simple answers and absolute clarity are bound to be disappointed.... There will always be a mystery"—Francis MacNutt. Scripture quotations could include Luke 4:18-19 and Luke 5:31-32.

As the class continues, individuals may wish to post more quotations.

Worship Resources

Hymn: "All God's Children," pp. 2-3, *Sisters and Brothers Sing!* (#1331, $4.00)*; "Living the Promise," p. 37, *In Accord: Let us Worship* (#3827, $3.95)*; "O For a Thousand Tongues to Sing," p. 1, "Sing Praises to God Who Reigns Above" (verses 1-4),† *The Book of Hymns;* "Te Vengo a Decir," p. 29, *Celebremos,* I

Prayer: Oh Great Physician, may your healing power be with us as we participate in this study. Touch our heads and our hearts with your hand. Open our eyes and our ears with your word. Give us your grace. Praise be to God. *Amen.*

Purpose

To begin thinking about the study theme of wholeness, healing, holiness, and wholeness of life.

Process

This unit can be done without a prior reading assignment to the group. Use it as an introduction to the themes in Luke which will be discussed in the text, as something to spark interest in continuing with the study.

---

†Please sing "all" or "folk" instead of "men" in verse four. In verse three, you may use feminine pronouns for God since the image is one of a mother.

Ask someone to read the foreword outloud to the group. Afterward you may wish to ask the following questions:

1. Does our local church (*unit*) take the total healing concept of church ministry seriously? Give examples.

2. Does our local church (*unit*) emphasize certain aspects of healing and neglect others? Give examples.

3. How might our church's ministry become more holistic?

Do not spend too much time discussing these. Indicate that these are questions to reflect upon during the entire study time.

This process may begin to move the group into sharing different definitions of healing and wholeness. Discuss some of the following questions or do some of the exercises.

Ask the group to do one of the following:

1. What does wholeness mean to you? Write down some words or pictures which come to mind.

(*After each person has done this, her or his response can be listed on the blackboard or newsprint for all to see. Ask each person to share one item at a time in order to give each person a chance to share information.*)

2. What does brokenness mean to you? Write down some words or pictures which come to mind.

(*Use a process similar to the question above.*)

3. How would you define healing? How would you define illness? Share your definitions with another person. Discuss similarities and differences between your definitions.

(*You may do the same with the words wholeness, holiness, and wholeness of life.*)

4. What would it be like to be a "whole person through Jesus Christ"?

5. If society were whole, what would it be like? Who would be included in it? Would anyone be excluded? Why or why not? What type of institutions would society have? What would be its basic values?

6. Share an incident in your life with another person in which you felt whole or experienced healing.

7. Give the class one to four index cards (depending on the number of responses you will request). Ask them to write their personal definitions of wholeness on the first side and to put their names in small letters in the upper right hand corner of the reverse side. Do the same process with healing, holiness, and wholeness of life if you wish.

Gather up the cards. At the last session of class, return the cards to them, name side up. Tell them not to look at the first side until they have written the definition of wholeness that now comes to them.

After partners have talked together, they may share some response about their learnings with the entire group.

Keeping a Journal: If members of the group are keeping a journal, ask them to place each of the three questions on p. 104 at the top of a new page. As ideas come during class sessions and reflection between the classes about one or more of these questions, they can write them down. At the end of the study, individuals can share their reflections if they wish.

STUDY SESSION II

Assignments

Reading: Chapter One in the text; Luke 1:1-3:21; 24:1-53 in the Bible

Art: Ask someone to draw the chart "What Is Its Structure?" in Chapter One large enough for all to see. Display it each time the class meets as a reminder of the structure of Luke.

(*You could also choose to project the slide on Luke's structure included in the Luke slide set.**)

Worship Resources

Hymn: "From All That Dwell Below the Skies," p. 14, "While Shepherds Watched Their Flocks," p. 394, *The Book of Hymns;* "Glory Be to God on High," p. 2, "The Right Hand of God," p. 50, *Songs of Zion;* "Las Posadas," p. 56, *In Accord: Let Us Worship**

Prayer: Dear God, we thank you for having come to us in human form into this world. You gave us a vision of how life can be. You showed special concern for women, for the poor, and the outcasts while still including men, the rich, and the powerful in your ministry. You announced the death of one way of living and the birth of another way—the way of love. In recognition of these things, we magnify your name.

Poems: "Magnificat," "Meditation on Luke 1," and "The Song of Zechariah." in *Image-Breaking/Image-Building* by Linda Clark, Marian Ronan, and Eleanor Walker, eds. (New York: The Pilgrim Press, 1981), pp. 72-75.

Purpose

To give a general introduction to Luke and a sense of Luke's vision.

Process

Choose one of the following options with which to begin class:

1. Ask the class the questions which are the major heads in Chapter One: What is the Gospel of Luke? Why was it written? When was it written? Who wrote it? How was it written? What is its viewpoint? What is its structure? What are its additional concerns?

Use this time to find out how much the class knows about Luke and to cover the information in Chapter One. If the class is too shy to answer the questions or seems to be floundering, you might assign each person at least one section of Chapter One to read in class and to report back on. This process will not take long.

2. Employ the lecture method to cover the general background information in Chapter One and show the

Luke Slide Set,* which is an overview of the Gospel of Luke.
Allow time afterward for questions and comments.

3. You could simply ask the group to share what it knows about Luke. Take its responses and expand them to include any information in Chapter One they may not have shared. A good technique would be to record the responses on newsprint, the blackboard, or on a transparency of an overhead projector.

4. Ask individuals to talk a little bit about their favorite story in Luke which relates to healing and wholeness. Each person should indicate how the story is about healing and wholeness.

5. Show the group the chart of the structure of Luke and discuss it. Note where most of the healing stories are within the structure.

After some general discussion, the class will be anxious to look at the Gospel of Luke itself. Following are some possible procedures.

1. What role in healing of individuals and society does vision play? What role did it play for Zechariah, Mary, Anna, and Simeon? What was the vision given to the disciples and others after the resurrection? What impact did it have? Must vision always emerge from pain?

2. What were the individual and societal situations out of which the visions of the people mentioned in #1 arose? In the early chapters of Luke? the last one? Do you think that a group's shared vision can alter the structure of individual's and society's lives? How? Can you give examples from your own life?

3. Write a poem, a song, a few paragraphs or draw a picture which expresses your hope for the future.

4. Why might Luke have decided to be so careful about opening his Gospel with complementary stories—one emphasizing a male, the other a female? What ideas would he have been trying to convey in his narrative? Read Luke 24. How does its message about men and women compare with that in the opening chapters?

5. Write a joyful song of praise to God or sing a hymn of praise which makes you feel joyful.

6. Chapters 1—3 of Luke describe the life of Jesus until age 30. Jesus participated in certain rituals at certain times of life. These rituals expressed the beliefs of his culture and marked different points in his life. Luke probably included them to show that his growing up was the same as any other Jewish boy's.

What are our rituals which mark different events in our lives? How do they contribute to a sense of wholeness in our selves, in our church, and in our society?

7. What are some rituals or disciplines that you practice that help to give you a sense of wholeness? (They may be something obvious such as prayer or less obvious such as tending a garden or doing dishes.) Pay attention to the rituals and disciplines that Jesus practices in Luke.

Keeping a Journal: Think of a societal problem which touches you, one by which you feel oppressed personally. It may be one of the "isms," such as racism, sexism, or classism. It may be something less global, such as being treated like an outsider because you weren't born in a particular area.

For the next week, write about your vision of how this situation can be changed. What must happen to you, to others? One technique to use before writing is silent meditation. Imagine the situation as it is, using a concrete example or a symbol to represent it. After you have a sense of the present situation, ask God to send a hopeful vision of future change. Write down what impression comes to you. Since the vision may be symbolic, spend some time reflecting on how its message might be incorporated into your life and society's. Do this exercise for at least three days. Probably, you will receive a different impression each time. Reflect on the combined meaning of all your "visions."

Then, if you wish, share your visions with others who have done the same exercise. How are your visions similar? How are they different? Can they be combined and made real in society?

STUDY SESSION III

Assignments

Reading: Luke 4:33-40; 5:12-26; 6:6-19; 7:1-23; 7:36-50; 8:26-48; 9:10-11; 9:37-43; 11:14-25; 13:10-17; 13:31-35; 14:1-6; 17:11-18; 18:35-43; 22:47-53. (These are 24 healing stories.)

Art: Ask someone to copy the chart "The Healing Stories in Luke" from the end of Chapter One in large enough letters for all to see. At least three sheets of newsprint will probably be needed. The person need not list the numbers under "text chapter."

Post a Bible lands map of the time of Jesus' ministry. (*Or the map from the Luke Slide Set* can be projected at the appropriate time of discussion.*)

Worship Resources

Hymn: "Gifts of Love," p. 106, *Sisters and Brothers Sing!*; "Open My Eyes, That I May See," p. 267, *The Book of Hymns* "Quien Es Ese?," p. 17, *Celebremos*, I

Prayer: Jesus, we stand in awe of the many healings of individuals and society that you performed in Israel. We witness to your continuing healing power which moves in the world today. Teach us to be whole persons. *Amen.*

Purpose

To introduce 24 healing stories in Luke.

Process

At the end of Chapter One, the author lists 24 healing stories in Luke. In class, assign each one to an individual or a small group to read and discuss. Some of these, such as the three labeled "Multitudes" (#5, 8, 16) are short, so you may wish to give them all to one person or group. Since #14 and #15 are joined together in the narrative, they may be taken by the same group, which can compare and contrast them. If the group is very small, you may not wish to assign all 24 stories.

One way to assign the stories is to ask each person or group to draw a number which corresponds to the number of one of the 24 stories which are listed in Chapter One and will be listed on the chart before them. Then they can look up the scripture which corresponds to it.

After the stories are assigned, ask the groups to answer certain questions and to report back on the "answers." Tell them that not all of the stories will provide answers for each blank. Use the chart below as a guide. These can be printed out on paper and distributed or listed on the blackboard or newsprint for the group to copy.

You could read the following answers to them as an illustration.

The Healing Stories in Luke

Scripture: Luke 4:33-37

1. Who was healed of what malady?

A man with the spirit of an unclean demon had it cast out by Jesus.

2. What was the setting?

It was in a synagogue in Capernaum, a city of Galilee, on the sabbath.

3. How did Jesus become aware of the person(s) who needed healing?

The man cried out in a loud voice. (He "made a scene"!)

4. What method(s) of healing did Jesus use?

Word—he rebuked the demon.

5. What was the response of the person after she or he was healed?

The scripture does not say.

6. What was the response of the witnesses after the healing? Why?

Amazement. They told others throughout the region about Jesus. Jesus spoke with such authority.

7. What is your response to the story? What did you learn about the healing ministry of Jesus?

(Enter personal responses.)

As the groups report in their charts, keep track of the different types of answers. Question 1 is essentially answered by the chart mentioned in the art assignment. Especially important for discussion will be Questions 3, 5 and 6. In relation to answers to Question 4, such as word, touch, faith, note that Jesus' methods of healing are a special emphasis of the study book. Tell the class that more time will be spent on this aspect later. Question 6 may provoke a discussion about why some were thankful and joyful and others were not.

Question 5 is an important one because the group will see a broad range of reactions from amazement, to joy and thankfulness, to reservation and questioning, to anger. Focus the discussion on this segment. Individuals may wish to reflect on how they would respond to these same events.

There is a historical explanation of the theology behind these reactions, but also there are very human ones. Often we assume that everyone wants healing and wholeness, but obviously people did not always react to Jesus in that way. Jesus performed these healings in a societal context and there was a societal impact. For some people, the changes he brought about through individual healings were threatening. He challenged some people's investments in keeping society just as it was. Some wanted people to be sick and poor, for instance, so they would have more control over them. Since individuals are a part of society, an individual healing changes the arrangement of society.

Lead the group in an exploration of contemporary movements working toward healing and the variety of responses the goal of healing has evoked. A number of examples can be discussed: choose one, such as the movements for peace and nuclear disarmament.

Conclude with the guided meditation "Healing" in *Wholeness in Worship* (#4031, $6.95),* p. 150. Instead of the passage in Mark, read Luke 6:17-19.

Keeping a Journal: For each day of the next 24 days, read a different healing story in Luke. Meditate on it for ten minutes and write down your reflections.

STUDY SESSION IV

Assignments

Reading: Chapter Two in the text; Luke 4:1-44; 9:1-11; 10:1-37

Report: Barclay, "Emissaries of the King," pp. 114-116; "Labourers for the Harvest," pp. 132-136; "Who Is My Neighbor?" pp. 138-141 in *The Gospel of Luke*, rev. ed.; Fisher, "The Parable of the Good Samaritan," pp. 72-74 in *The Parables of Jesus* (#3388, $1.50)*

Worship Resources

Hymn: "Live Into Hope," p. 90, "When I Needed a Neighbor," p. 102, "The Good Samaritan," p. 131, *Sisters and Brothers Sing!*; "Hope of the World," p. 161, *The Book of Hymns*, "Yo Tengo Paz y Gozo," p. 10, *Celebremos*, I

Sing the antiphon for the Song of Mary in "Mary's Song" by Diedra Kriewald in *Through It All... God: Program Resources* (#4067, $1.50),* pp. 51-53 as a part of worship.

Poem: "Go Tell Everyone" by Mother Teresa in *The Healing Fountain* (#1218, $1.45),* p. 57

Meditation: "On Healing" by Paul Tillich in *The Healing Fountain,* p. 114

Purpose

To gain an understanding of Jesus' concern for ministering to both the body and soul of persons and to apply these understandings to developing a holistic Christian ministry today.

Process

Begin with reading the fourth chapter of Luke, concentrating on 4:16-20 in particular. Ask the group to read it and interpret it. Look up Isaiah 61:1-2 and compare the two passages. Read the Magnificat and see how the song anticipates the ministry of Jesus.

Read the following quotation and discuss it:

> The poor, captives, the blind, the oppressed: These are the groups listed in this passage. In the light of the meaning of these verses in their original context, there are good grounds for holding that it is the literally poor and literally blind who are

designated. Reference to several other passages in Luke's account also leads us to believe that when Luke refers to the poor, the blind, and so forth, he means those who are literally poor and literally blind.[1]

Ask questions such as:

1. How do you feel about Cassidy's insistence that the passage be interpreted literally? Are you more able to accept a literal interpretation of the societal healing part than the individual healing or vice versa?

2. What would it mean if we accepted this passage literally and tried to carry out a similar ministry?

Then ask the class to read 9:1-17; 10:1-37. Discuss:

3. What were the areas of ministry to be done by the disciples and the seventy?

4. After recording the story of the mission of the Twelve, Luke wrote down the story of the 5,000. What type of ministry is demonstrated in this passage? Why might an author put these two stories next to each other?

5. How were the ones sent out to determine when to stay and when to leave? How do you feel about the attitude they were to express when persons rejected them?

6. Why were they to carry nothing with them?

7. What were the ministries the disciples and the seventy were to receive?

8. Look at 10:5-6. What is it saying about the nature of peace? Have you ever wished someone peace who did not want peace? How did you feel? Did the peace come back to you or did you feel angry or experience some other emotion? What did you learn about your deeper commitments to peace? What did you learn about how peace comes to the world?

The text mentions that Luke is the only Gospel which contains the Parable of the Good Samaritan, which teaches about ministry to both physical and spiritual needs. Read Luke 10:25-37. Note that Luke placed this story and parable shortly after the story of the seventy.

9. Ask the group to list the things which the Good Samaritan did to minister to the man who had been robbed. How was

---

[1]Cassidy, p. 22.

he a neighbor to the man?

10. Look at the risks which the priest, Levite, and Samaritan would have had to take to help the man. What were they? What are the risks involved in ministry today?

The discussion about Jesus', the disciples', and the Good Samaritan's ministries can lead into a discussion of a holistic ministry and of the terms *shalom*, *soteria*, and *nephesh*. You could begin with the following quotation from Betty Pagett, a United Methodist minister in California:

> When I think of healing, I think of the Hebrew word *shalom* in the sense of not perfection or illness but the sense of wholeness and woundedness. Healing, to me, is a sense of completion and of strength that can come from the ending of brokenness, the re-membering of oneself in body or in spirit. I think all ministers are involved in healing. I don't see healing in the old image of faith healers who advertised that they were available to heal but in the everyday practice of ministry. I feel I am involved in healing. I feel I am involved in healing when I visit shut-ins and people in the hospital, of course, most obviously. I'm also involved in the healing of old and ancient wounds in relationships between people.[2]

The class could discuss her definition of *shalom* as it is applied in contemporary ministry.

Choose some activities from those below:

1. Discuss the meaning of *shalom* and *soteria*. How might these ideas be applied to our lives today?

2. Discuss the meaning of the Hebrew concept of *nephesh*. How do you think about the human person? Do you think one part (either the soul or the body) is more important than the other? Why? Can you think of examples when Christians have emphasized one part of the person more than another rather than as a body-soul unity in their ministry? Can you think of examples when this emphasis has been balanced?

3. If we were to believe human beings are a living *nephesh*, what type of ministries would we develop?

---

[2]Interview given to Nancy A. Carter, December 15, 1981.

4. Say "hello" to people trying to convey its original spirit of conveying health and wholeness to the person addressed.

5. What was the Greek healing tradition of Asklepios? What are some valuable parts of the tradition which we could put in use today?

6. Read the six reasons of illness given by Basil the Great. Do you agree with all of these? Are there any you would subtract? Any that you would add?

7. Think about various societal illnesses. Do you think any of these reasons would apply to them? Are there additional reasons?

Keeping a Journal: As you read Luke, note times when Jesus treats people as body-soul units. Write down your reflections on these passages.

STUDY SESSION V

Assignment
Reading: Chapter Three in the text; Luke 7:1—8:56; 18:35-43

Worship Resources
Hymn: "O For a Thousand Tongues to Sing," p. 1, *The Book of Hymns;* "Amen," p. 16, "Faith Is Such a Simple Thing," p. 72, *Sisters and Brothers Sing!**

Prayer: Most gracious God, give us the gift of faith. Show us the path of trust. Cast out our fears. We pray this in the name of Jesus Christ.

Purpose
To look at four healing stories in Luke (7:1-10, the centurion's slave; 7:36-50, the woman of the city; 8:43-48, the woman with the flow of blood; and 18:35-43, the blind beggar) and focus on the relationship between faith and healing.

115

Process

Many persons believe that faith is an essential part of healing and that the Bible supports this notion. They will be surprised to learn what the Bible actually says. For some, the idea of the healing grace of God will be a relief from the idea of "faith healing." Others will wish to support the "faith healing" idea. One important question will be "whose faith?" In the story of the Centurion's slave, the Centurion and his friends had faith. This is third party faith. The faith of the slave is not mentioned. In the stories of the woman of the city and the blind beggar, the ones to be healed had faith but not the witnesses.

A misuse of the idea of healing through faith is to blame the one seeking healing for lack of faith if a healing is not perceived. The group may wish to talk about this. Another misuse is to tell the person who has been to a healing service that she or he must throw away needed medicine and have faith that healing has happened. Experienced healers know that humans cannot predict the healings God's grace will bring. Since the type of healing cannot be predicted, persons must consult with a doctor for confirmation of the healing of a physical illness.

Note the number of questions in boxes in the text's chapter and plan to use all or some of them.

1. Ask the class to read Luke 7:1-10. This story concerns healing by word and authority. Another means of healing is present— intercession of friends. Looking at this story may lead into a discussion of the importance of community of faith to healing work. Ask the group if Jesus ever comes in contact with the centurion's slave. It will probably quickly say no. Then ask if Jesus ever meets the centurion. Some may say yes. Then ask them to read the story again. The elders intercede for the centurion. Jesus never directly meets Gentiles in the Gospel of Luke.

2. Why did Jesus think that the centurion's faith was so great? Who might be a centurion today in relation to the Christian faith?

3. What is faith? Make a collage of words and images which come to mind.

116

4. If faith is not essential for healing to happen, what might be?

5. Read Luke 18:15-17 and 18:35-43. Why would some people try to keep others from being healed by Jesus? How do our churches today try to prevent children from coming to Jesus? How do they prevent persons with handicapping conditions from coming? Who are others who are barred?

6. How do perseverent faith and God's grace still enable healing, not only of the seekers but of those who erect the barriers to Jesus?

7. How does our society keep people from "seeing" today?

8. What do you choose to see and not to see when you drive through a city slum or a rural poverty area? When you see a "shopping bag lady"† in the city or a small town "drunk"? Could you ask Jesus to heal that blindness? Why or why not? Does anyone keep you from seeing? (Do not be afraid to admit that you may want to keep your blindness and to tell why.)

9. In the story of the woman of the city, Jesus tells the woman "'your faith has saved you; go in peace!'" (8:49). How did she demonstrate her faith?

10. Were you surprised to discover that only four of the 24 healing stories in Luke mention the idea of faith as healing? Why or why not?

11. Conduct the worship service "Casting Out Our Fears" in *Wholeness in Worship*,* pp. 111-117.

Keeping a Journal: Choose a place indoors or out of doors. Sit down quietly and close your eyes for ten minutes. Pay attention to what is around you. What do you "see"? Write down your observation.

Ask a friend to lead you on a "trust walk" while you are blindfolded. Write down your experience.

---

†A homeless woman who carries all of her possessions with her in shopping bags.

STUDY SESSION VI

Assignment

Reading: Chapter Four and Five in the text; Luke 4:40—6:49; 9:28-36; 11:1-13; 13:10-17; 18:1-4; 22:47-53

Worship Resources

Hymn: "Give Me Your Hand," p. 36, "Give Me Your Hand," p. 50, *In Accord: Let Us Worship;* "He Touched Me," p. 72, *Songs of Zion;* "Re-Member Me, p. 86, "Jesus, You Are With Us," p. 88, *Sisters and Brothers Sing!*

Poem: "Not for the Hesitant," p. 130, *Images: Women in Transition* (#2796, $4.95)*

Prayer: (*Stand or sit in a circle and hold hands. Pray silently for the healing of an individual and/or society.*)

Purpose

To experience the healing power of touch and prayer.

Process

This session and the next one may evoke discomfort in your group. People tend to have strong feelings, either negative or positive, about laying on of hands and prayer and healing in general. Some may have been hurt by abusive practices in healing. Others may have experienced a physical healing and now fanatically insist that people be healed the same way as they have. Some may be skeptical. Others may have experienced healing but are afraid to share it with others for fear they will be thought to be strange or naive. Still others, of course, will see the larger picture which healing involves. Try to create a supportive atmosphere in the group which will enable persons to share their experiences without trying to dogmatically force their viewpoints on others.

Healing happens in many ways. Ellen Klemperer, a Quaker who is founder of the Howard Thurman Listening Room Movement, has said:

> Healing takes place whenever the love of God, either directly or indirectly, touches the individual's or a group's mind, body

118

and spirit enabling God's whole-making force, energies, to do their holy work. In this sense, then, healing is inherent in all of life, assuming that life itself wants to be whole, wants to be one (as indeed it is, I believe, at its essence) wants to be complete.

As God is infinitely inventive, so healing can come through an incredible number of ways, ways which the healer—him or herself—may be only vaguely conscious of. The healed may not realize what is happening.

I think of Jesus' reference to a cup of cold water given in the Spirit of the Lord. I think that a smile passing a stranger on the street may bring healing. To me, the recognition of the sacrament of the total life and the trying to act on it releases healing to everything, to every thought for thinking has its own power and can work either for good or for disruption.[3]

Discuss the discomforts often felt about laying on of hands and prayers for healing. Make sure people understand that healing is not "magical" but is an everyday process that we sometimes do not even recognize. Healing services formalize or ritualize this process and often speed it up, but they are not the only means of healing.

1. When are you comfortable about touching or being touched by people? When are you uncomfortable? Why?
2. Discuss the benefits of touch.
3. Do the benediction in *Wholeness in Worship,** pp. 100-101. It involves using the word *shalom* with different body movements, including touch.
4. Make a list of Francis MacNutt's four types of healing. Then find all of the healings described in the reading assignment for this chapter and see if you can categorize them in one or more of these categories. Do they seem to work? Are there other categories?
5. Write down or reflect on a healing in your life. What type of healing was it? How did it come about? Was it gradual or instantaneous?
6. How can prayer be a life-style? What is action-oriented prayer?
7. Pray for healing of another, yourself, or society. One type of healing prayer is to imagine the person to be healed as

---

[3]Interview with Nancy A. Carter, October 12, 1981.

being bathed in white light—the Light of God or Jesus. If you are praying for an institution, society, or the whole world, choose a symbol to represent it and imagine it is bathed in white light.

8. Do "A Service of Healing" in *Wholeness in Worship**, pp. 145-147. Before having it, you will want to discuss it and do some reading, such as *Wholeness in Worship, Healing,* and *Power to Heal.*

Many people have been "harmed" rather than "healed" when the purpose and results of healing services have been abused or misunderstood. The Emswilers, who affirm the validity of healing services, also warn: "This whole area is fraught with dangers. People's expectations may be raised in unwise and invalid ways. Lack of obvious healing may make some question their faith. Healing services are often associated with a naive theology, and irresponsible leaders tend to take advantage of people already weakened by illness and pain."[4] Remember that usually healing is not instantaneous (like its television image) but is a gradual process. Always trust that, even if healing is not visible to human observation, God is bringing about healing in some way in a person. There is no cause for despair or blaming the person who seeks healing for lack of faith when results are not readily apparent. Also we can not predict what type of healing will take place. We may ask for a physical healing and receive an inner healing. All healing services are done in the spirit of God's love, not in the spirit of judgment.

Design the service so that it will be low key and will focus on the healing power of God. Take care that the services don't focus on individual's personal experiences. Testimonies can be uplifting, but sometimes people can get too carried away with talking about the past and fail to focus on present concerns for healing, or they will focus too much on themselves and not on God (even though they say they are giving God the praise). Also groups tend to have one person who wants to monopolize all of the time and who therefore

---

[4]*Wholeness in Worship* (San Francisco: Harper and Row, 1980), p. 48.

120

alienates others. Read instead a healing story in the Scripture.

Keeping a Journal: For the next seven days, write a prayer for healing: 1) for yourself, 2) someone else, 3) your family, 4) your local church, 5) your denomination, 6) the United States, 7) the world. Pray the words and follow it with silent meditation. As time goes along, note any changes in any of these which seem to be related to God's healing power. Were some prayers easier to write than others? Why?

STUDY SESSION VII

Assignment
Reading: Chapter Six and Seven in the text: Luke 4:31-39; Luke 9:1—10:20

Worship Resources
Hymn: "Spirit of the Living God," p. 39, "Sweep Over My Soul," p. 40, "Blessed Are Those," p. 70, *Brothers and Sisters Sing!**
Prayer: We confess that we have been guilty of being rich, full, happy, and popular without concern for the poor, hungry, mourners, and outcasts. Forgive us. We ask your blessing. Help us to understand what it is to lay up riches in heaven as we live daily. *Amen.*

Purpose
To reflect on how we perceive our world and to focus on the power of words and the Word in life and their influence on our view of the world.

Process
Different people see the world in different ways. Our perceptions of the world influence our attitudes toward it, our interpretations of events, and our actions. This session provides an opportunity to examine our world-views

through a discussion of different biblical and contemporary opinions about demons and of the power of words to shape reality.

If people in your group differ in their opinions about demons, you will have a lively discussion. Take care that no one is made to feel demeaned or ridiculous because she or he has a different opinion. Also take care that if members of your group believe in demons that they not get carried away with the idea. Refer to the precautions in MacNutt's book *Healing*. Note that even if demons do possess people, it is very rare indeed. Often what people label "demons" is their own fear projected on another object or person. Neither the object nor the person is "demonized."

1. What were the different world views of Jesus' time which were behind belief (or lack of belief) in demons in Jesus' day? Describe these views (Apocalyptic, Jewish-Gnostic, Greek-Orphic).

2. Read Luke 8:29-39. Why do you think the Gerasenes were afraid and asked Jesus to leave? Why did the man who had been healed ask to be with him? What was Jesus' response?

3. Discuss your feelings about belief in demons. How would you explain the biblical accounts? Is your viewpoint similar to the Apocalyptic, Jewish-Gnostic, or Greek-Orphic one? How does your perspective affect the way you live your life?

4. Can institutions be "demonic"? In what ways? Does this mean that the individuals involved in that institution are "evil"? Why or why not?

5. What was different about the words which Jesus used when he spoke?

6. Read Luke 5:17-26. This is the famous Sermon on the Plain. Who is to be blessed? Who will encounter woe? Compare the Sermon on the Plain with the Beatitudes.

7. What power does the word in form of a sermon have?

8. What power do words have today? Your words? Printed words?

9. How do words shape our reality? Select printed material on a controversial topic which comes from different perspectives. Look at the different terms which are used to

describe the same persons (such as "cripples" or "persons with handicapping conditions"; or "perverts" or "gay men and lesbian women," or "niggers" or "Blacks"). Think about how "blessings and curses" work today.

10. Discuss the various theories of the source of the power to heal which are presented in Chapter Seven. What do you believe?

11. What was the characteristic reaction by those healed in the Gospel of Luke? How about in the Gospel of John? Why were the reactions different?

Keeping a Journal: Draw a picture or write some words which represent a fear, or a "demon," or a curse in your life. Put this on a page which has no writing on the back. On a second page, write about how you have experienced this fear, how it has disabled you. Then decide what you want to do with the drawing on the first page. Do you want to keep the fear or banish it? Create a simple ritual which expresses this wish. (For instance, you might burn the page and say "be gone!" as it goes up in smoke.) After performing your ritual, return to your journal and write your feelings about the experience.

STUDY SESSION VIII

Assignments

Reading: Chapter Eight and Nine in the text; Luke 1:8-25, 57-66

Art: Make a chart on paper or the blackboard which lists the old Hebrew, late Jewish, and Greek views of malady and gives a little explanation of them. Include information such as the name, examples of it in scripture, belief about the origin of malady, and attitude toward malady. For the Greek view, it is important to know that some scholars think that the tradition of Asklepios influenced how Jesus is

portrayed as a healer in the Greek scriptures. The influence
of this model on the Judeo-Christian tradition comes later
than the first two but is also important. Today all three
models are adhered to totally or in part by people, so they
should provoke thought in your group about its beliefs
about sickness.

Worship Resources
Hymn: "Amazing Grace," p. 92; "Balm in Gilead," p. 212,
The Book of Hymns
Prayer: Divine Healer, we gather in this place with the
knowledge that all of us have been wounded at one time or
another in our lives. Some of these wounds have healed;
others have not. Give us balm for our wounds. If our
wounds must remain for a while, give us endurance and
insight, so that even our illnesses can enable the healing of
ourselves and others. *Amen*.

Purpose
To discuss the relationship between wellness and illness
in individuals and society and different theories about this
relationship including ideas about "law" and "grace."

Process
For some, these two chapters will be the hardest to read.
A lot of historical information and scholarly opinion is
given. Because of their placement in the text, the chapters
are taken together here but "The Role of Malady" could be
combined with "The Role of the Word" and "Technique or
Grace?" with "The Role of the Healer" if the class doesn't
mind reading chapters out of order.
1. What is malady? Is it evil? Is it good?
2. How was malady caused according to the old Hebrew
view? Read Luke 1:8-23, 57-66, 4:23-26; 5:17-27 as examples.
What was the cure of malady in this view? How was it
caused in the late Jewish view? Read Luke 21:5-28 as an
example. Which of these views supports the idea of
demons?
3. What was one Greek view of malady? Are there scriptural
examples of this viewpoint? How can someone be a

"wounded healer"? What is the view of shamanism? How can illness be "a necessary part of a person's development"?

4. Hand out cards with everyday statements which reflect one of the three views of malady. Ask the individuals to read these cards out loud and to discuss which view they represent and why. This may help them to understand the chapter better. Possible statements are:

Why did God let this happen to me?

Is God punishing me for something?

The flood was an act of God.

I'm sorry that your child was killed by a car driven by a drunk driver. I know that God suffers with you.

I know you are upset because you are a minister and are now divorced, but this experience will help you to understand others in similar situations.

People are poor because God is punishing them.

People are poor because the system is evil; let's get rid of the system.

People are poor because God is teaching them spiritual values.

People will no longer be poor in God's New Age.

5. What is the relationship between illness and wellness? For further reflections, read *Wellness: Your Invitation to Full Life* (#4213, $5.95).*

6. What is the function of pain in healing? What are the three responses to this question that Joseph Fichter has noted are often given?

7. How do these views of the problem of evil relate to visions of the new age?

8. What is grace? What Greek word is it taken from? How does healing relate to grace?

9. What are the drawbacks to a too rigid belief that faith heals, such as blaming a sick person for lack of faith if she or he does not get well? Have you known people who believe this?

10. What are the two graces? Which view(s) of healing (see above) does the idea of the grace that heals seem to go with? the grace that enables endurance?

11. Discuss the theories about healing which are presented

at the beginning of Chapter Nine. Whose views are closest to yours?

12. Review the meaning of *shalom* and *soteria*. How do these relate to a theory about how healing happens?

Keeping a Journal: Draw a time line of your life. Mark the periods when you suffered some emotional, spiritual, or physical sickness. Write about three of these. Reflect on the following questions. What was happening in your life at the time? What was happening in the nation and the world? Was there a cause for your malady? If so, what? Was your life changed after the sickness; did you view life differently? How? Were others involved in your healing? Did faith and prayer play a role in the healing? If you still suffer from the illness, how do you view it? Have you been given the grace that endures? Does the malady somehow enable you to be more whole in another part of your life?

If you perceive your malady to have been linked to events in the nation or the world, was your healing related to a healing in the nation or the world? If your healing has not happened or has been partial, do you think it is still linked to a societal ill? Do you think you will be healed before society is? If so, how might your healing influence that of society?

STUDY SESSION IX

Assignment

Reading: Chapter Ten in the text; Luke 1:46-55; 4:16-19; 6:20-36; 7:18-23; 7:36—8:3; 8:40-56; 10:38-42; 12:13-34; 16:1-5; 18:1-14, 18-30; 20:45—21:4; 24:1-53

Worship Resources

Hymn: "In This Lan'," p. 11, "Behold the Man," p. 58, *In Accord: Let Us Worship**; "Lord Jesus, Friend of Women," p. 129, *Images: Women in Transition**; "We Are Gathered," p.

12, "Male and Female," p. 13, "Mine Are the Hungry," p. 91, *Sisters and Brothers Sing!**; "Come Sinners to the Gospel Feast," p. 102, *The Book of Hymns*
Meditation: "The Silent, Hungry Ones," *The Healing Fountain**, pp. 82-83

Purpose

To explore Luke's special concerns for the poor and women and relate individual wholeness and societal wholeness.

Process

The class will have already discussed a number of passages, such as Luke 1:46 and 4:16-19. Review these earlier discussions noting that Luke's interest in the poor and in women is established early in the gospels. These themes are woven through the Gospel. Using the examples of the poor and women, links can be made between individual and societal wholeness.

As you begin, you may wish to start with the following quote from Susan Savell, a United Church of Christ minister who is a healer, songwriter, and singer in New York City.[5]

> Healing work takes so many forms. In my view, it's just as important to be a healer of the whole society as of the individual. Working as a healer of the whole society and of the individual are two sides of exactly the same coin that many of us will probably weave in and out of for the rest of our lives. I really don't see any separation between those two roles. I don't see any separation between the healing of the individual and of the society because the individual is so connected to the whole social fabric and the social fabric of the society so determines the health of the individual.

Or you may wish to begin with this one from Sharon Neufer Emswiler, a United Methodist minister who wrote *The Ongoing Journey: Women and the Bible** and co-authored *Wholeness in Worship:*[6]

---

[5]Interview given to Nancy A. Carter, Spring, 1982.
[6]Interview with Nancy A. Carter, December 8, 1981.

Healing is a political act. As individuals become more whole, particularly as women become more whole, it changes their relationships to themselves and the men they're related to. It changes their relationship to society as a whole. Some people see this as being a detrimental thing, upsetting the status quo, making people uncomfortable in these changes. It may be like the surgeon's wound that's necessary before healing can take place. We can't have a whole society—one that is healthy—and have women who are sick and wounded. Before the society can be well, the individual members of it have to be well too. I think that feminism has been a path of healing for women and myself.

1. How does healing happen in society? Can social action bring about healing? How? Can social action impede healing? How?
2. Think of an example of individual and societal healing being closely linked together.
3. How does an individual become whole? How do we move toward wholeness?
4. List some sickness in society. Choose one of these and pray for its healing.
5. Read the following quotation from Cassidy's *Jesus, Politics, and Society*:

> Although Luke's Jesus is strongly concerned about the poor, he does not offer any explicit analysis of why they were poor. At first, this might not seem to be the case, given the frequency with which Jesus criticizes the rich and admonishes them to give up their surplus possessions. However, when we reflect over the full range of Luke's reports, we see that there is scarcely an instance in which Jesus has charged the rich with exploiting the poor or has indicated their actions have helped to maintain or create poverty. To be sure, Jesus challenges the rich to use their surplus possessions to provide for the poor and implies that they are negligent if they do not, but he does not assign to them any responsibility for the fact that the poor are poor.

Cassidy says that Jesus "manifested a strong and consistent concern for the poor"; he often asked those with

---

[7] Cassidy, p. 32.

surplus possessions to use them to benefit the poor; and asked the disciples to "find ways to enable the poor (and the infirm) to participate fully in the ongoing life of the community" (14:12-14). An important feature of Jesus' general response to social suffering was the theme of "an inclusive community or society."

Ask the class to discuss whether or not it agrees with Cassidy's interpretation of Luke. Why or why not? Ask them to turn to passages such as Luke 6:20-26; 12:13-34; 16:1-13; 16:19-31; 18:18-30; 19:1-10; and 19:11-27. Do these passages seem to support Cassidy's view?

6. In the text, Lindsey Pherigo mentions the story of Mary and Martha (10:38-42). He says, "Perhaps what Mary was doing met a deeper need in Jesus than what Martha was doing. One can only wish that the story included Jesus' affirmation of Martha as well." Read the story and ask the class to discuss their feelings about Jesus' treatment of each woman. If the class likes skits, encourage some spontaneous versions of the story allowing them to change it if they wish. Discuss reactions to the differences between the skits and the story in Luke.

Keeping a Journal: Become quiet. Find the "center" in yourself. Where is it? What is it like? Are others present? Can it aid you in becoming whole? Write your reflections immediately upon finishing.

STUDY SESSION X

Assignments

Reading: Chapter Ten in the text; Luke 15:1-32 in the Bible
Report: "The Joy of the New Age" in Neal Fisher's *The Parables of Jesus: Glimpses of the New Age* ($1.50),* pp. 55-63

"The Shepherd's Joy," "The Coin a Woman Lost and Found," and "The Story of a Loving Father" in William Barclay's *The Gospel of Luke,* revised edition, pp. 199-206.

"Retrieving the Lost" in G. B. Caird's *Saint Luke,* pp. 179-184.

Worship Resources

Hymn: "Parables," p. 62, "Go Now in Peace," p. 128, *Sisters and Brothers Sing!**; "I Sought the Lord," p. 96, *The Book of Hymns*, "Toma Por Favor," p. 27, *Celebremos*, I

Purpose

To examine the idea of wholeness which is in chapter 15 of Luke and relate it to our own experience of wholeness and health.

Process

William Barclay has said, "There is no chapter of the New Testament so well known and so dearly loved as the fifteenth chapter of Luke's gospel. It has been called 'the gospel in the gospel,' as if it contained the very distilled essence of the good news which Jesus came to tell."[8] A study of this chapter can be a good way of summing up the entire study. The three parables in it all reveal a concern for the whole, for completion. All 100 sheep are important, all 10 coins, the unity of the family. Exercises involving one or more of these scriptures could be used.

1. Read Luke 15:1-32. Who are the "lost" in our society? Who are the ones who must be included to make it whole but are excluded by the "older brothers" of our day? Who are those who are lost by "accident," and who is searching for them? Who are those who have gone astray and are asking for help? Do we want to find them?
2. Read Luke 15:11-32.
   a. Role play the parable and complete the ending—does the older brother rejoice or remain stubborn? Let the group discuss its reactions to the ending chosen. Was it realistic? What feelings did it evoke? Which son was the lost son? Why?
   b. Hold court. Ask Father, Younger Son, Older Son to state their cases why the younger son should or should not be welcomed into the family. Discuss your reactions.

---

[8] Barclay, p. 199.

3. Get a small poster board or stiff piece of paper. Draw a circle. Place ten coins on the circle equally distant from each other. Ask the group to reflect on their feelings about the design and write them down. Then take one coin away. Ask them to write down their feelings. Replace it. Ask them to write down ther feelings again. Then the group can share its experience.

As a variation, you might try a variety of types of coins one time and identical coins another time. Is there a different reaction, especially if the coin you remove is different from the others?

Read Luke 15:8-10 and discuss it.

4. Think of a part of yourself that you have "lost" that you would like to find again. Imagine that you are searching for it. Can you rejoice when you find it or is there a part of you which rejects that lost part?

Think of a part of yourself that you have lost and would not like to find again. Can you find some good in it that needs to be re-discovered? Do you need to somehow reclaim that lost part?

5. Ask the class to join hands in a circle and to feel what it is like to be in the circle. Each might imagine that she is a coin in the Parable of the Lost Coin or a sheep in the Parable of the Lost Sheep. Then ask someone to leave the circle and the room as the "lost coin" or "lost sheep." Let the group discuss its feelings about wholeness and brokenness. Ask the separated person to return and to talk about her feelings about wholeness and brokenness. Take some time for silent reflection. Then read the poem "A Circle" by Anita Wheatcroft in *Images: Women in Transition** (p. 69) or *Live the Questions Now: The Interior Life** (p. 108).

It is possible that this exercise can evoke strong emotions in people. As a leader, be prepared to direct the group in loving support. Loving support does not mean taking away the pain or avoiding conflict but helping the group to honestly struggle toward wholeness.

6. Do the worship service "The Empty Space" in *Wholeness in Worship,** pp. 94-101.

7. Adapt the ritual "Search for the Lost Coin" in

Image-Breaking/Image-Building (pp. 48-49) and use it to conclude the course.

8. If you did exercise #7 in Study Session 1, you may wish to repeat it here. Hand out the original cards and ask them to write on the side where the name is. Then they can discuss any differences and similarities between their first and their last responses.

9. Hand out two paper or cardboard discs three or six inches in diameter. One is a "lost" coin. The other is a "found" coin. On one coin, each is to write down something that she or he has lost during the time of the study; on the other, something found. (Examples: "I lost my fear of......; I found a new understanding of healing; I lost a belief that was very important to me.") Ask them to tape their coins to two large sheets of paper, one labeled "lost" and the other labeled "found." Look for similarities and differences. These may become part of a worship service.

10. As part of the conclusion or follow-up to this study, discuss matters such as: What were the most important learnings from this study? Has there been a progression toward wholeness in this group? If so, can we carry it further into our community and beyond? What are our future plans for individual group work in the areas of wholeness and healing?

Keeping a Journal: Make a list of some losses, significant and less significant, which you have experienced during your life. Choose three of them and answer the following questions. What was your reaction when you experienced the loss? Did you feel as if a part of you was missing? Did you find it again? If so, how did you feel? Did your attitude toward the lost thing change? If you did not or could not find it (as in the death of a loved one), how did you feel? Were you able to re-achieve a sense of wholeness? How?

SHORTENING THE STUDY SESSIONS

Six Sessions

I.

Assignment: Do the reading listed for Study Sessions I and II in the guide.

Process: Choose one of the shorter exercises on defining healing and wholeness from Session I. Show the Luke slide set.* Discuss the general outline and content of Luke. Look at one of the passages which is a vision or song and discuss your own visions of wholeness.

II.

Assignment: Do the reading listed for Study Session IV.

Process: Choose material from this session.

III.

Assignment: Do the reading for Study Sessions V and VI.

Process: Discuss laying on of hands and prayer including the "faith healing" concept. Focus on some of the healing stories mentioned in the sessions, especially the woman with the flow of blood, Jairus' daughter, and the blind beggar. You may wish to adapt the chart exercise in Study Session III as a means of looking at these stories more carefully. Use one of the worship suggestions for Session VI.

IV.

Assignment: Do the reading for Sessions VII and VIII.

Process: Look at the concept of a world view and link it to ideas about demons, malady, and the use of words.

V.

Assignment: Do the reading for Study Session IX.

Process: Select material from this session.

VI.

Assignment: Do the reading for Study Session X.

Process: Select material from this session.

Four Sessions

I.

Assignment: Do the reading listed for Study Sessions I, II and IV.

Process: Choose one of the shorter exercises on defining healing and wholeness from Session I and relate the ideas to the definitions of *shalom* and *soteria*. Discuss the general outline and content of Luke. Study Luke 4:16-20 using helps from Study Session IV.

II.

Assignment: Do the reading for Study Sessions V and VI.

Process: Show the Luke slide set.* Discuss laying on of hands and prayer including the "faith healing" idea. Focus on some of the healing stories mentioned in these sessions.

III.

Assignment: Do the reading for Study Sessions VII and VIII.

Process: Look at the concept of a world view and link it to ideas about demons, malady, and the use of words.

IV.

Assignment: Read Chapter Ten of the text and related scripture.

Process: Use the process in either Study Sessions IX or X. If doing the former, choose something from the latter to give the class a sense of completion.

Glossary

Apocalyptic: An adjective derived from the Greek noun *apocalypsis*, which means "revelation." It is principally used to describe a literary type (books or writings like the Book of Revelation) or a type of theology (theology like that in the Book of Revelation). "Apocalyptic Judaism," therefore, is a type of Judaism that expresses itself like the forms and theology of the Book of Revelation.

Apostasy: Going from a believing to an unbelieving stance, going to disloyalty from a former loyalty. Our word comes from a Greek word meaning to desert, abandon, or revolt from.

Before the Common Era (B.C.E.): See Common Era.

Common Era (C.E.): A more inclusive way of dating historical events than the older, more provincial way in use among Christians since the seventh century—B.C. for Before Christ and A.D. for *Anno Domini* (the year of Our Lord). Christians today are becoming more aware of the feelings and convictions of Jews and others who do not place Jesus Christ at the focal point in history. Using C.E. (Common Era) and B.C.E. (Before the Common Era) demonstrates this respect without in any sense diminishing a Christian's loyalty to Christian theology.

Etymology: The study of word origins and the history of changes and developments in the meanings of words.

Hellenistic Jews: Those Jews who adopted the language of the Hellenes (Greeks), and, in varying degrees, their cultural ways also. All the writers of the New Testament were Hellenistic Jews, except (probably) the author of the Book of Revelation. The emergence of the term "Christians" as the special name for those Jews who believed in Jesus Christ is noted in Acts 11:26. Elsewhere in the New Testament, even in Luke-Acts, what we now call "Christians" are called "believing Jews."

Incubation: The practice, common in antiquity, of seeking healing from a supernatural source by sleeping overnight in the sacred precincts of the particular supernatural power. In Egypt, temples of Imhotep (the Egyptian god of healing) were incubation centers. Among the Greeks, Asklepian shrines functioned similarly. The practice carried over into some areas of Christianity.

Irenaeus: Bishop of Lyons in Gaul (France) during the last quarter of the second century C.E. He is generally regarded as the first great Catholic theologian.

Jewish-Gnosticism: Gnosticism viewed the universe as a prison

and the material world as the source of all evil. Humans were sparks of God imprisoned in a physical body. Both God and human inner selves were purely spiritual and alien to this universe. Salvation involved knowing this true God, knowing oneself to be part of God, and therefore being rescued from this prison-world. This saving knowledge (*gnosis*) was imparted by a redeemer figure who was "not of this world." Jewish Gnosticism modified this by accomodating (with difficulty) the concept of God as Creator, but in none of our sources is this accommodation ?
satisfactorily explained. *Makes sense to me.*

Luke-Acts: the term coined in modern scholarship to describe the untitled 2-volume work now separated in the New Testament under individual titles, the Gospel of Luke (volume I) and the Acts of the Apostles (Volume II). The overall unity of the two volumes is easily established. Neither volume can be fully understood without the other.

Shalom: the Hebrew word of customary greeting, meaning healthy, sane, whole, complete, peaceful, safe. In Arabic, "salaam." In Germanic languages it has no exact equivalent, but parallels the German "heil" and the Anglo-Saxon "hal" or "hale." The common English translation "peace" is much too restricted to convey the full meaning of *shalom*.

Soteria: The Greek word usually translated "salvation." It means much more than salvation in the usual religious sense. It includes salvation from poor health and from all kinds of dangers and threats. It is a rescue word and includes very positive meanings of being rescued *for* something as well as *from* something. No English word translates all its meanings.

Theophilos: The addressee of the two-volume work Luke-Acts, as indicated in Luke 1:3 and Acts 1:1. Because of the honorific title in Luke 1:3, the Greek word is probably the name of an otherwise unknown official in the government of the Roman Empire. A minority opinion sees the word as referring to anyone who loves God, since the word itself is a Greek word meaning "lover of God," or "friend of God."

Weltanschauung: a German word expressing one's understanding of how human existence fits into the universe at large. "World-view" is a literal, but incomplete, way to translate it. Since English has no adequate equivalent word, it is commonly left in its German form when precision of thought requires what it says. The French "milieu" is closer than the English "environment."